Letts EXPLORE

I'm the King of the Castle

Susan Hill

Guide written by
Stewart Martin

A *Letts* Literature Guide

Extracts from *I'm the King of the Castle* by Susan Hill are reprinted by kind permission of the author.

First published 1994 by Letts Educational Ltd,
Aldine House, Aldine Place, London W12 8AW

Text © John Mahoney and Stewart Martin 1994

Typeset by Jordan Publishing Design

Editorial team Rachel Grant, Wayne Davies

Self-test questions devised by Sandra Lissenden

Text Design Jonathan Barnard

Cover and text illustrations Hugh Marshall

Graphic illustration Ian Foulis and Associates

Design © BPP (Letts Educational) Ltd

British Library Cataloguing in Publication Data
A CIP record for this book is available from the British Library

ISBN 1 85758 265 9

Printed and bound in Great Britain by
Ashford Colour Press Ltd, Gosport, Hants

Letts Educational Ltd is the trading name of BPP (Letts Educational) Ltd

■ Contents

■ Plot synopsis

Joseph Hooper is a middle-aged widower who lives with his young son Edmund at Warings, their ugly old Victorian family house, following the death of Mr Hooper's parents. Mr Hooper has advertised for a housekeeper and a friend for Edmund and as a result of this Helena Kingshaw (a widow) and her son Charles arrive at Warings near the start of the summer holidays. Edmund Hooper resents their arrival. The two boys, who are both about eleven years old, fight each other almost as soon as they meet and it is clear that their relationship will continue to be stormy.

Whilst exploring the countryside around his new home, Charles Kingshaw is attacked by a huge crow. Edmund Hooper witnesses this and taunts Charles about his cowardice, daring him to go into the nearby woods and forests alone in order to prove he is not a coward. The same night Hooper leaves a huge stuffed crow on the bed of the sleeping Kingshaw, who is terrified but refuses to let Hooper know that he has frightened him. The following day Hooper shows Kingshaw around the Red Room, which is full of dead moths that his grandfather collected over many years. Realising that Kingshaw is frightened by the dead creatures, Hooper locks him in the room. Later that night Kingshaw prays that Mr Hooper will ask him and his mother to leave Warings. He misses the familiar surroundings of his school.

Kingshaw finds an unused room on the top corridor of the house and adopts it as his secret escape from Hooper, keeping it locked. Eventually Hooper finds the room and demands to look inside, where he finds various items that Kingshaw has collected. Hooper realises that Kingshaw is planning to run away because he is afraid of him. He tells Kingshaw that he will not let him run away and that he will follow him. Meanwhile Mrs Kingshaw and Mr Hooper are developing a close relationship and think that their boys are also getting on well together.

During a visit by his mother to London with Mr Hooper, Kingshaw runs away. He is followed by Hooper, who refuses to leave him, into Hang Wood. During the course of the day they wander into the much larger Barnard's Forest and realise that they have become lost. There is a thunderstorm, which terrifies Hooper. The boys find a stream and follow it to a clearing with a pool, where they spend the night. Hooper becomes hysterical at the thought that no one will ever find them. Whilst Kingshaw is looking for a way out of the forest, Hooper falls into the stream and knocks himself unconscious whilst trying to catch a fish to eat. He is saved from drowning by Kingshaw, who returns and takes care of him as night falls. During the night Kingshaw is awakened by screaming as Hooper has nightmares. The following day they are found by a search party of men with dogs.

Hooper tells everyone that Kingshaw is to blame for their running away and for his own injuries. Hooper's versions of events always seem to be believed by the adults, and Kingshaw grows increasingly resentful because of this. Kingshaw also senses that his mother understands nothing of his feelings about being at Warings and is made more unhappy by his suspicion that she and Mr Hooper have grown so fond of each other that they will marry.

Mr Hooper announces that Kingshaw is to attend the same school as his son. Kingshaw despairs at the thought that he will not return to his old school, which is the only place where he has felt happy. He hides in a shed in the allotment, but Hooper locks him in and terrorises him with suggestions about the insects and animals that he says live in there. He adds that he will make sure that all his friends make Kingshaw's life miserable at his new school.

Mr Hooper takes Mrs Kingshaw and the boys to visit the ruins of Leydell Castle. Kingshaw, who loves climbing at school and is unafraid of heights, scales the walls and dares Hooper to follow him. Hooper climbs part of the way up but becomes afraid and will not move. Kingshaw tries to help him but Hooper falls. He is taken to hospital. That night Kingshaw has nightmares, thinking that he has killed Hooper, and goes downstairs. There he learns that Hooper will survive and Mr Hooper carries him back to bed.

During Hooper's hospitalisation Kingshaw makes friends with Fielding, a local boy, with whom he shares some of his problems. But when Hooper returns, the old hostilities flare up again. Kingshaw is taken to London by Mr Hooper to get the uniform for his new school. On his return he finds Hooper playing with a model he had designed and built. When he complains about this, Mr Hooper slaps him.

After partly overhearing a telephone call between Mrs Kingshaw and an old friend, Mr Hooper decides that he has not been decisive enough in his relationship with Mrs Kingshaw. Mr Hooper takes everyone to the circus, but Kingshaw, who has always been terrified by the circus, is violently sick. Later, Mrs Kingshaw tells her son that she has invited Fielding to tea. Kingshaw is angry because Fielding will meet Hooper, and so won't be his private friend any more. Fielding finds himself in the middle of the tensions between the two boys, and finally invites them both to his home to play, to escape from the uncomfortable atmosphere. Kingshaw cannot bear to share his visits to Fielding's home with Hooper, so he stays at Warings. While the two boys are away, Kingshaw destroys the battle charts on which Hooper has been working.

Mr Hooper and Mrs Kingshaw plan their wedding for the same day as the return of the boys to school. Kingshaw realises that he cannot face the future, especially as he receives a note from Hooper warning him that something is going to happen to him. Kingshaw leaves the house early next morning and makes his way back to the clearing and pool in the forest. There he drowns himself. His body is discovered by Hooper, who feels triumphant that Kingshaw has killed himself because of him.

Characters and themes in *I'm the King of the Castle*

Mr Hooper

A widower who has inherited the family home Warings, Joseph Hooper has a difficult relationship with his son, Edmund. He feels that his life has so far been a failure.

Mrs Kingshaw

Helena Kingshaw, the widowed mother of Charles, her only child. She is employed as housekeeper by Joseph Hooper at his house (Warings) but later agrees to become his wife.

Edmund Hooper

The eleven-year-old son of Joseph Hooper. He persecutes Charles Kingshaw and eventually drives him to his death. He seems motivated purely by evil.

Charles Kingshaw

The eleven-year-old son of Helena Kingshaw. Most of the action of the novel is seen through Charles' eyes. He is relentlessly persecuted by Edmund Hooper until he finally drowns himself.

Anthony Fielding

The eleven-year-old son of a local farmer, who befriends Charles Kingshaw. He is a cheerful boy who is well-known and well-liked locally. He has an open and natural approach to others, which contrasts to both Charles and Edmund.

Childhood

Childhood

 Evil

Evil

 Isolation and loneliness

Isolation

 Love

Love

 Nature

Nature

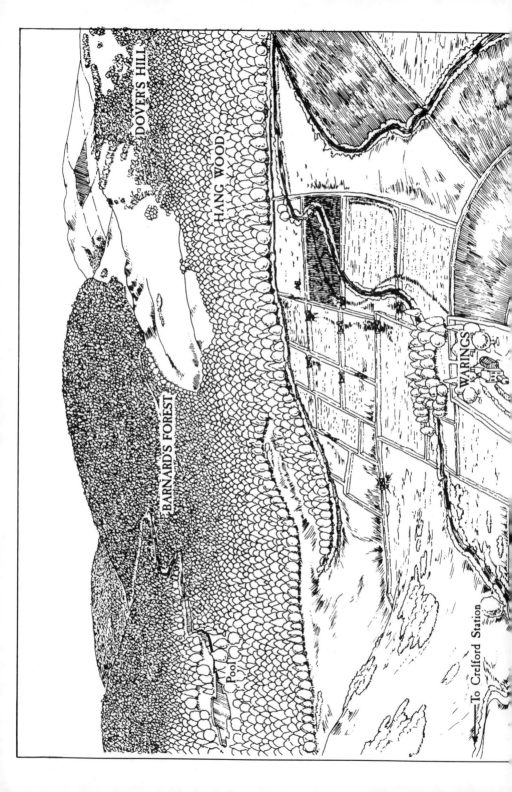

Old
tin shed

N

FIELDING'S FARM

Village of
DERNE

Mr Hooper

Mr Joseph Hooper

Mr Joseph Hooper is fifty-one years old, but looks older. He is a thin, pale-faced man with receding hair and a small, pursed mouth. An ineffectual man who lacks imposing qualities, he is, by his own account, a failure in life, and admits to himself that he is lonely. He knows himself to be a dull man, who 'gets by' in life but leaves no impression. He has moved to the family home Warings and finds its depressing but imposing character encourages him to acquire in his middle age a 'dynastic sense' – a feeling of being one of a line of leaders in a great family.

He boasts of the other family heirloom – the moth collection – but actually hates it. This collection is Mr Hooper's father's legacy. It is symbolic of death and emotional rigidity: the grey corpses of the moths are drained of life and beauty, as is the Hooper family. The lack of colour and life in the moths collection is echoed by the Hoopers' skeleton-like bodies and pale complexions, and the way the cold light of the moon floods the rooms of the house and the surrounding landscape.

Mr Hooper tells his son Edmund to show respect for his grandfather but knows that he is able to show it himself only now that his dying father 'is almost gone away'. Mr Hooper feared his own father but it seems unlikely that his own son feels anything at all for him. His father made Mr Hooper watch him work on his collection of moths and butterflies in the Red Room. Mr Hooper thinks that Edmund is like his mother Ellen, with whom Mr Hooper obviously had a difficult relationship. Although she has been dead only six years, Mr Hooper finds it hard to remember what his wife looked like.

He is not ashamed to admit his loneliness to himself, but he is also timid, and is alarmed at his own action in placing an advertisement for a housekeeper. When Mrs Kingshaw arrives, he becomes desperate that everything should please her. He knows himself to be an intensely sexual man whose passions cause him to sweat in his sleep as he dreams excitedly of women. He is aroused at the sight of the female trapeze artists at the circus, with their swinging and arching bodies. He remembers his marriage as being 'polite' and it is clear that his wife did not satisfy his physical appetite. Mrs Kingshaw becomes an outlet for his lust and he feels pleasure in her company, as well as pride and satisfaction that she is relieved to be at Warings. He is convinced that she will respond to his physical desires without the 'niceties and the restraints' which his wife demanded. He feels sure that she recognises his physical needs and that she has similar longings, although we have no evidence of whether this is true.

Although he admits that he is lonely, Mr Hooper seems to have little real interest in other people as individuals. For example, he spends the train journey into London telling Kingshaw about the sights, ignoring the fact that Kingshaw used to live there. By the same token, he seems unsettled by fact that Mrs Kingshaw has had a life of her own before meeting him, as when her telephone conversation reminds him that she has a past he knows nothing about. Mr Hooper mistakenly thinks that 'boys are very simple animals' and becomes smug in this new–found confidence. He wonders whether he has exaggerated the unhappiness of his own childhood because of his recent bad patch caused by the death of his father and the move to Warings. Certainly he reveals no understanding of what is really going on in the lives of Charles and Edmund.

Mr Hooper has tried to avoid his own father's mistakes in bringing up his son but he has only replaced them with his own. He finds his own son arrogant and insolent and blames his wife for dying without leaving the rules for dealing with him. He is uncomfortable about his lack of understanding of his own son, but reveals that he himelf loathed his father at Edmund's age. Interestingly, he likes to think of himself as normal in this respect. He tells Mrs Kingshaw that he will make no distinctions between the boys, but given how little he understands his own son this is not much of a promise and is unintentionally ironic. He finds Kingshaw easier to deal with than Edmund because there is nothing 'strange' about him, unlike his own son, of whom he is clearly afraid. Although he slaps Kingshaw when he feels he has misbehaved, he never disciplines his own son, although he wishes he could. For his part, Kingshaw thinks of Mr Hooper as some kind of crow or 'terrible bird'. Edmund reveals that his father goes about clutching a large bunch of keys and this, together with the gloomy atmosphere of Warings, suggests the image of a jailer.

Mrs Helena Kingshaw

Mrs Kingshaw is a rather prim thirty-seven-year-old widow who is Charles' mother. Feeling past her prime, she is making an effort to 'catch' a husband. She never mentions her past husband, and Charles remembers him only dimly. She is not very wise about the real world, prefering to live in a world of her own, where happy endings always happen. She is permanently anxious that everything should go well and turn out all right. Since her husband died she seems to have struggled to support herself and Charles, taking poorly paid jobs and having no permanent home. She has managed to keep Charles at his private school only because he has a scholarship, which pays towards the cost.

She tells her son that her position at Warings is the answer to their prayers, so things must not go wrong because this is 'her chance'. She is absolutely determined that they shall all be happy, and does not want her son to spoil everything. Hers is not a strong personality and she is 'ready to be full of interest and admiration' when Mr Hooper is around. Whether she enjoys this is unclear, and you may feel that – given the high stakes – she feels she has little choice. She sees it as her job at Warings to say the right things and look at ease. She never seems to talk as a mother to her son about any of the changes in his life, not about Warings, moving schools, or even about her proposed marriage to Mr Hooper.

Mrs Kingshaw is very concerned about appearances – although her son is not. Charles hates the way she increasingly wears too much make-up around Mr Hooper. This explains the importance she plays on what people say and the way they speak. For example, she tells Kingshaw several times not to say 'OK'. She plays a cat-and-mouse game with the telephone call from her friend because she knows Mr Hooper is listening, and her comments about not being sure what she would like to do with her future are directed entirely towards him. By the use of this device she attempts to manipulate events.

Mrs Kingshaw seems convinced that she is a good mother because she says and does all the 'right' things, like always going to kiss her son goodnight. But in fact she is condescending towards her son and never listens, or gives any sign of wanting to listen, to him. She believes Hooper's story about Kingshaw hurting him in the woods by pushing him in the water. Similarly, Hooper's guess that she'd rather be with him than her own son seems to be at least partly correct. She repeatedly betrays her own son in pursuit of her own happiness. Her blindness, ignorance and foolishness contribute to his death. Ironically, she feels that she does not think of herself enough.

Mrs Kingshaw is completely unaware of what is really going on between the boys. Her description of Hooper as Charles' 'special friend' contains an irony of which she is unaware. When Charles tells her the way he really feels about Hooper, she dismisses it as, 'silliness and a little bit of shock after the accident'. Such things are the measure of her lack of understanding of her own son. But her behaviour towards him reflects her desperate attitude to life – she thinks that repeatedly saying things are a certain way will somehow make them so.

As time goes by – especially after Hooper's fall – she alters in how she speaks to her son. A sharpness enters her voice as she changes her behaviour to please Mr Hooper, to show she is not favouring her own son. She decides to take more care of her appearance, again to please Mr Hooper. This is partly the reason why she takes sides against her own son when he is slapped by Mr Hooper. She allows Mr Hooper to take them all to a circus even though she knows it will make her son feel ill. When the circus makes her son physically sick she tells him off, saying that he should have said something, or just waited.

Mrs Kingshaw desperately wants someone to lean on – before coming to Warings she appears to have used her son this way, but now leans on Mr Hooper. She feels a sense of security, a sense of 'arrival', about the coming wedding to Mr Hooper. She is sure of her future happiness and that 'everything is about to begin'. For her son these same words signal the coming of fear, persecution and terror beyond bearing. We learn nothing of her thoughts as she looks upon the body of her drowned son. All we hear are her words to Hooper: 'I don't want you to look, dear, you mustn't look and be upset, everything is all right.' She is unaware of the irony of her words, for Hooper's actions have produced this sight and he feels triumphant about it. But her words summarise her attitude to life – she has always avoided looking clearly at things, especially when they are upsetting. It seems unlikely that she will ever recognise the blame she carries for her son's suicide.

Edmund Hooper

Hooper

Hooper is almost eleven years old and is a pale, thin-necked boy with square teeth which have a gap between the front two. He is the unloved son of Mr Joseph Hooper and is an isolated, but not lonely child. When we first meet him, we are told that he is 'never afraid' as though it were a simple truth. But this is not so, as we learn when he becomes terrified during the scenes in the wood and at the castle. Hooper is unable to love others: at the start of the book he thinks of his dying grandfather as something which resembles one of his dead old moths. His father seems to have neglected him – notice how Hooper feels that it is nothing new that his father is away from home in London for much of the time after they move to Warings. His bedroom is high up at the back of the house, overlooking the copse – he prefers this 'narrow room with a tall window' which gives an aerial view of the world below. The description of Hooper's room makes it sound almost like a coffin. The view from his room makes the outside world look like one of his model landscapes of battlefields. He is physically distant from the world and people outside.

Hooper's first response when he learns of the arrival of Kingshaw is that Warings is his house, it is private, and when the new boy comes he will 'not give anything of himself away'. This is a good description of Hooper's approach to life: he is a taker, not a giver. He is uncommunicative and sends notes to Kingshaw right from the start, rather than talking to him openly. Even his threats to Kingshaw are usually vague. When Kingshaw arrives, Hooper thinks he sees why it is better to have a house like Warings – somewhere private which belongs to him.

Sometimes Hooper behaves like a very small child – for example, when he sticks out his tongue and breathes heavily while crayoning and colouring in. When he sleeps in the forest, he curls up like a foetus with his thumb in his mouth. We are given few insights into Hooper's thinking during the course of the book, which makes his character difficult to understand.

In spite of his callous dismissal of Kingshaw's mother and the way she shows affection to her son, Hooper is the one who has terrified dreams in the forest and screams out 'Mummy! Mummy! Mummy!' Yet there seems to be no real evidence of envy in Hooper's spitefulness about the way Kingshaw's mother kisses him good night, no evidence that Hooper is missing his own mother – certainly not during the daytime. He is pleased when Mrs Kingshaw comes to see him in hospital, even though he does not like her much, because he thinks it means she'd rather be with him than with Kingshaw. Hooper tells Kingshaw that fathers are better anyway, although he has no affection for his own father. His father cannot control Hooper and feels that only his mother was able to deal with him. Hooper himself remembers nothing at all of his mother. He behaves like someone who has never known the genuine love of a father or mother. He is angry when he learns his father is to marry Mrs Kingshaw because it means Kingshaw will stay and he is powerless to stop it.

Although Hooper makes much of his status at school, he reveals that he is allowed to go out of class to lie down if it thunders. We might wonder whether he is in fact highly regarded by the other boys. His nightmare in the forest had something to do with having a blazer, and may well echo an incident where he was bullied. We see no evidence of the many friends Hooper says he has at school.

Hooper is a relentless and patient persecutor of Kingshaw. He surprises himself at the 'charm' this cruelty to Kingshaw affords him – he is filled with excitement at the idea of terrorising him with the stuffed crow, for example. Hooper is essentially a cowardly person – he is afraid to go and look at the animal the boys hear in the wood and makes Kingshaw do it. He covers his fear with boasts, as when he pretends to Kingshaw that he knows everything. This is exposed for the sham it is on a number of occasions, as when he thinks bears and boars live inside the wood. He is a physically timid boy (notice how he soon becomes wary of Kingshaw's fists), so we might wonder why he follows Kingshaw into the wood. He behaves as though tormenting Kingshaw is an addictive habit which he cannot give up.

He tells Kingshaw: 'There are things I see that you don't'. This is true in more ways than one, for he sees ways to torment Kingshaw, to lie to the adults and to win every time, which baffles Kingshaw. He is purely spiteful, as when he locks Kingshaw in the shed. Hooper is the one who finds Kingshaw's body in the pool, 'because he knew at once where he would have gone'. He feels triumphant that Kingshaw kills himself because of him. Hooper seems to be, as the author Susan Hill says, purely evil and persecutes Kingshaw in an obsessive way, for no other reason than that there is nothing to stop him.

Charles Kingshaw

Charles Kingshaw is the son of the widowed Mrs Kingshaw. He is almost eleven years old. Contrary to the folklore that red-haired people have fiery tempers, he is not by nature an aggressive or confident boy. Kingshaw feels permanently vulnerable, so prefers to get on with people at almost any cost because it is safer. He knows that he is the sort of person who is no good at competing, only at plodding along by himself. He does not see himself as cowardly but as realistic – he feels that he will always be beaten by other people and so his own view of himself protects him from surprise or disappointment. He thinks of himself as the sort of person whose name other people forget.

Kingshaw is upset by the way things have to change so often – he wants things to stay the same. He blames his mother for bringing them to Warings, ashamed of her, because he suspects Hooper is right when he taunts Kingshaw about her seeking a husband by 'going after' men. For the same reason he remembers being embarrassed at his school speech days when his mother arrived wearing her 'slippery-looking dresses and too much jewellery and make-up'.

Kingshaw seems to want very much a 'normal' mother and family and he is envious of Anthony Fielding for having a mother who appears natural, loving and genuine. He feels strangely comforted by Mr Hooper's arms when he carries him up to bed after Kingshaw wakens from a nightmare. This longing for a loving family probably explains his annoyance when his mother gives Hooper presents. It also explains why he feels cold and dead the first time he goes in the forest and fears that neither his mother nor Mr Hooper will want to come and find him. Kingshaw admired and wanted to be friends with the boy Fenwick at his school, because he was strong and tough when he fell and gashed his knees. Kingshaw feels that he can never be like that.

To Kingshaw, adults seem to decide everything without asking him: the move to Warings, the change of schools, the trip to London for his uniform, his mother giving Hooper his model fort, the wedding between his mother and Mr Hooper. He feels that his mother betrays him by arranging for Fielding to come to Warings without telling him. After Hooper falls from the castle walls, we read: 'what Kingshaw remembered most clearly was being ignored'. He often feels like this, as though he is not really there.

He begins to feel sick with shame at the way his mother speaks to Mr Hooper, and wants to spit 'great gobbets of phlegm into his face'. He reminds himself that things were no better before they came to Warings. Then his mother would cling to him and say he was all she had and that she wanted so much for him to do well. Kingshaw knows that the 'weight of meaning behind her words' is that he has to carry her future as well as his own, and he feels that this is too big a burden. He thinks that his mother has never really known anything about him at all.

Kingshaw is frustrated by Hooper's ability to control situations – even though he realises that this only happens because he is allowed to. Hooper is, he knows, clever, inventive and unpredictable, but he senses that Hooper is only just learning to be a bully. Kingshaw feels powerless to defend himself in the face of Hooper's lies about what happens in the forest and the way the adults believe them. When Hooper puts the stuffed crow on his bed Kingshaw knows that it is dead, but that only makes it worse somehow – he is afraid of what it might do to him. His fear that moths might land on his face at night has been with him since he was young. Kingshaw fears the unknown, and all other hidden threats. To him, the implied violence of a TV film is more frightening than actual violence. His memories of all the odd places he and his mother have stayed include a private hotel and a peculiar old woman who lived in one of the rooms there. Again his fears about her are more imagined than real. He is happy when Hooper is in hospital and he is left alone in Mrs Boland's care because he doesn't have to think of anything terrible to come.

When Hooper locks Kingshaw in the old shed it is not the dark which frightens him and makes him physically sick, but the thoughts and pictures that pass through his head – the nightmare of Punch and Judy turning into crows and Punch's skull being broken open and bleeding. He cries in the darkness of the shed because there is no other relief. In the shed he dreams of running towards the light at the end of a long tunnel while being chased by things which are dragging him back. When he reaches the end he falls over a cliff towards the water which comes rushing up to meet him. This is a nightmare vision of the future: his hopes of escaping the darkness of Hooper's persecution end in the water of the pool in which he drowns himself.

Hooper's menace is psychological. All Kingshaw feels he can do in response is to conceal his thoughts from Hooper as best as he can. Kingshaw has never hated anyone until he hates Hooper. This worries Kingshaw, because he believes people are punished for bad thoughts. He feels guilty about the malicious thoughts he has about Hooper and asks for forgiveness for them in the church. But Kingshaw also believes that evil thoughts can be used to inflict punishment, so the fact that Hooper seems to wish him ill has a powerful effect on him. Again, Kingshaw thinks that Broughton-Smith wished his warts onto him because he did not like him.

Kingshaw knows that Hooper's power is not a physical one: rather, it comes from reminding Kingshaw of his own fears. In contrast, Hooper is terrified by external threats: heights, thunderstorms, being lost or left alone in the forest. But Kingshaw's fear comes from within and is therefore ever-present. The battle with Hooper is continuous and Kingshaw never feels as though he wins, even when he does. The live crow which attacks him at the start of the book treats him as prey, just like Hooper does.

When Kingshaw climbs the walls at Leydell Castle, he feels strong and safe because he is beyond the influence of others. But Kingshaw never uses his advantages over Hooper, even when he is in a position to kill him on the castle walls. Kingshaw is not afraid of heights, the loneliness of the forest or the prospect of wild animals which so frighten Hooper – in fact, these things excite and please him. He can cope with physical difficulties and physical things because he is resourceful. Note that it is Kingshaw who runs away; Hooper merely follows, like a malignant spirit. Hooper would never have entered the wood alone. Even Fielding is wary of the woods.

Kingshaw's longings for freedom revolve around the world of nature: terrifying though the wood is, it is safe. He is interested in the family of wrens in the alder bush near where he goes to see the squirrels and has a desire to hold one of them in his hands – a desire for the freedom they have, like the freedom he gave back to the rabbit he caught in the wood. His intense care for other creatures is in contrast to Fielding's matter-of-fact approach to farm life. On the farm Kingshaw is overwhelmed by the many 'terrible truths' about the way the animals are killed. Unlike Hooper's attitude towards dead things (whether moths, rabbits or people) Kingshaw feels that dead things do matter. In spite of everything that Hooper has done to him, Kingshaw is even afraid that Hooper will die after he bangs his head. Kingshaw puts himself through mental torment about this. He cannot think of leaving Hooper alone in the forest and feels responsible for him.

Kingshaw feels pleased when he has Fielding as his own special friend. But he becomes depressed when he cannot 'own' Fielding exclusively, because Fielding is the sort of person who will make friends anywhere. When his mother arranges for Hooper to meet Fielding it is 'the last thing' for Kingshaw. He feels deprived of a private life. He is depressed by the unfairness of the fact that Hooper cannot make Fielding afraid. Hooper knew, from the first moment he looked into Kingshaw's face, that he could make Kingshaw afraid. Kingshaw admires the way Fielding dismisses the things in the Red Room, saying only that they 'smell a bit funny'. Kingshaw wants to go with Fielding when he invites them all to see his new tractor, but he can't because it won't be like it was before – Hooper has spoiled it all. When a message appears under Kingshaw's bedroom door, saying, 'Something will happen to you, Kingshaw', he knows it is from Hooper and realises: 'people are no good, then, people can never help me.' When Kingshaw awakens at dawn, he realises what he has to do. He is excited when he returns to the wood – it is his place, the only place where he now feels comfortable. At the pool he hesitates for a moment, but then lies down with his face in the water and takes a long breath.

Fielding

Anthony Fielding

Fielding appears late in the novel, but is important for the contrast he makes to the other two boys. The son of a local farmer, Fielding is small-faced and brown as a nut, and has long eyelashes which to Kingshaw seem as long a spiders' legs. He is friendly with everyone and liked by the local people. He is refreshingly normal when compared to the two other boys in the novel. He meets Kingshaw in church, makes friends with him and invites him back to his home. Unlike Hooper, he is always careful not to push Kingshaw into anything he doesn't like – he invitates Kingshaw to watch a cow calving not to test Kingshaw's courage, but because he thinks it is something which Kingshaw might find interesting. Fielding's reaction to the calving is different to Kingshaw's. He does not share Kingshaw's intense feelings of sympathy for individual animals. He explains in a matter-of-fact way how the turkeys are killed, seeing the violence as a necessary part of farming life.

Fielding tries to help Kingshaw by saying that he should not be afraid of people like Hooper, but his advice is lost on Kingshaw because he does not share Fielding's natural confidence. Fielding is a straightforward individual and does not know how to react to the tensions between Kingshaw and Hooper, because he does not understand them. Unlike Kingshaw, Fielding is naturally immune to the kind of treatment which Hooper deals out to Kingshaw, as Hooper himself seems to realise.

■ Themes and images in
I'm the King of the Castle

Themes are the important ideas that run through the novel. You will come across them lots of times. They connect together the characters and the different parts of the story.

When words and descriptions suggest a picture in your mind, that is called an **image**. Images are often used to make an idea stronger, or to encourage you to think of things from a particular point of view. If you described someone as being 'as skinny as a stick' or as behaving 'like a wild animal' you would be using images. Many of the examples you will find in the novel are striking, but others will be more subtle, so you will need to pay careful attention to the language that Susan Hill has used. The following notes will help you.

Childhood

Childhood

Although the book is about children, it was not written for young people. But the book has proved popular with them, perhaps because it highlights the difficulties of coping with childhood. Many of the sentences are short, mimicking the way children speak. Adults often have a romantic view of what their childhood was really like – a view coloured by memory. To them the book is often shocking, because it paints such a black picture of the lives of almost all the characters, especially the young Kingshaw and Hooper. The impact of the book is increased by an ending which seems somehow inevitable.

The book deals with the feelings of helplessness which children often have in the face of bullying and cruelty. Just as Kingshaw's mother and Hooper's father fail to understand their children's relationship, so Kingshaw cannot understand why Hooper behaves the way he does. Hooper is almost impossible to understand, partly because his evil defies our ability to understand it.

The young Kingshaw struggles unsuccessfully to deal with ignorance, indifference, a lack of love and the presence of evil. As this seems to be the way many young people experience childhood, the book succeeds in what Susan Hill has said is the main job of a writer – to make people realise that they are not alone.

Evil

Evil

Evil is a strong feature of the story and displays itself mainly in the psychological violence of Hooper towards Kingshaw. Physical violence is often portrayed as a normal part of life – as on Fielding's farm – or as a normal part of the young boys' relationship. This violence of nature or of farm-life is seen as distinct from the notion of 'evil'.

Hooper's evil defies understanding because we do not know what drives it – the reasons he gives seem somehow inadequate to explain his relentless persecution of Kingshaw or his feeling of triumph at Kingshaw's death. Kingshaw is unable to understand Hooper's evil any more than Mr Hooper can fathom his son's thoughts. The book is not religious in any sense and Hooper's evil is not seen in from any religious point of view. The evil we see is secular. Ignorance, stupidity and lack of love allow evil to triumph, not the absence of religion.

For evil to triumph all that is necessary is that people should not care for each other. Neither Mrs Kingshaw nor Mr Hooper seem willing to take the trouble to get to know their children. To Mrs Kingshaw, her son seems an encumbrance, even a threat to her future happiness. The nearest she comes to any recognition of evil is when she scolds her son for his 'wickedness', but in reality she is conscious only of childish naughtiness. Mr Hooper senses something about his son which makes him uneasy, even frightened, but does nothing to deal with it. The lack of any real love allows the evil in Hooper to grow unchallenged. There is no redeeming motive for Hooper's evil actions. His tormenting of Kingshaw is done for no other reason than that he wishes to behave this way – it gives him a strange pleasure. One of the reasons many readers dislike the book is that evil is seen to triumph. Uncomfortable though it may be, the ending is true to the the experiences and feelings of many younger readers.

Isolation

Isolation and loneliness

Several different kinds of isolation are in the book. Mr Hooper and Mrs Kingshaw are the adult parts of two single-parent families. Warings itself is set apart from the local village, which is itself isolated. None of the characters have significant contact with the village, although it is mentioned several times.

The house and the nearby woods symbolise the characters' psychological isolation from each other. In the same way, each of the main characters is separated from people with whom they might once have had relationships – Mr Hooper's wife is dead, like Mrs Kingshaw's husband, and young Kingshaw has been separated from what he regards as his proper home and from his school friends. Mr Hooper feels isolated from his own past and from his inheritance, Warings, and hopes somehow to 'grow into' these things. Edmund Hooper seems to have no anchor in past relationships. He tells Kingshaw that he has many friends at school, but there is no evidence of them, whereas Kingshaw receives cards from his school friends.

There is little communication between Hooper and his father, or between Kingshaw and his mother. Communication between Mrs Kingshaw and Mr Hooper seems to be confused, each interpreting the behaviour of the other to mean different things. Neither show any sign of wanting to enter into a meaningful relationship; neither seems to like, far less love the other. Mrs Kingshaw thinks marriage to Mr Hooper will give her stability and security; he thinks she will give him sexual fulfilment.

Mr Hooper is wary of communication with son, feeling that he is strange and too much like his mother. Mr Hooper's relationship with his past wife was far from successful. He therefore resents his son's similarity to her and sees him as, like her, cold and hard.

Mrs Kingshaw never wants to hear what her son says, so he has given up trying to explain his problems to her. She sees things as she wants them to be and uses words and expressions to create her particular view of reality. Her keenness not to favour her own son above Hooper leads her virtually to ignore Kingshaw. Her over-anxious approach to everything widens the gulf between her and others. For Kingshaw, the one person who should be his greatest ally becomes a stranger to him.

Love

Love

With the exception of the Fielding family, there is no love in *I'm the King of the Castle*. However, apart from Edmund Hooper, all the characters are desperately searching for a loving relationship. Different characters have come to different conclusions about what they think will complete their lives: Charles Kingshaw was keen to leave his mother when he went to school and seems to have missed her only slightly. He is comforted when Mr Hooper carries him upstairs to bed and does not want to be put down, yet later is embarrassed by his own feelings.

Mr Hooper seems to have some feelings of kindness towards Kingshaw, but is fearful of his own son. His past wife found his sexual demands tiresome and his interest in Mrs Kingshaw, like his fascination with the acrobats at the circus, seems to revolve entirely around his lust for sexual fulfilment.

Mrs Kingshaw seems irritated by her son and anxious that his behaviour should not 'spoil things' for her. She is trying to escape from the difficulties with which she has had to struggle since her husband died and this colours the way she treats everybody else. Her behaviour towards others is governed less by natural affection than by the importance she places on 'proper' behaviour and on having a secure future.

Fielding is the only character who is secure in the natural love of a family and is therefore invulnerable to the stresses which plague most of the other characters. Except for Edmund, the other characters are searching for what they feel they lack. But it is suggested that the four central characters are unloved and unloving. As the story unfolds it seems unlikely that any of them will ever be able to give or receive love in a straightforward way.

Nature

Nature

The novel is set in a rolling, rural landscape. The action opens at the start of summer and closes at the start of autumn. The events are set against changes in the weather and in the seasons, and against incidents which occur in the world of nature. In contrast to the natural beauty of the landscape, the house, Warings, is brutally ugly and dismal.

One side of nature is seen as actively violent – like the crow which attacks Kingshaw. There is also local fear of the ominously named Hang Wood, and of the darker and more threatening Barnard's Forest. Kingshaw picks up a dead rabbit which is a rotting mess of worms inside, and

Hooper watches intently as a thrush kills a snail. But the violence of nature seems without malice, unlike Hooper's vendetta against Kingshaw.

The crow is an interesting exception to this because for Kingshaw it becomes a symbol of evil. It attacks him, apparently for no reason, as he walks through the fields. The crow becomes identified with Hooper, who at times looks crow-like to Kingshaw, as does Mr Hooper. The crow appears in Kingshaw's nightmares, and in stuffed form is put on his bed by Hooper, to torment him further. The other creature from nature which becomes a symbol of terror for Kingshaw is the moth. Kingshaw has never liked moths and has an irrational fear of them landing on his face. He dislikes the thought of their smell and their dusty, fluttering bodies. It is significant that Hooper's visit to the Red Room culminates in his destruction of a Death's Head moth, which crumbles into dust in his hands. Hooper therefore becomes identified with symbols of the terror of death and of the night. But these are symbolic connections only – the other animals which Kingshaw meets never frighten him – he feels only pity and affection for them.

It is not violence itself which frightens Kingshaw – what frightens him is when violence is deliberately directed at some creature, or himself, with the intention to harm. He is upset by the way the farm animals are raised only to be killed, and sees this as different from the violence in nature. Kingshaw is not sure about the violence surrounding the birth of the calf – he feels overwhelmed by the knowledge of it. The violence of natural events is more frightening to Hooper than it is to Kingshaw. The world of nature is shown as safe from human cruelty, which is why Kingshaw feels at ease in the woods. Kingshaw longs to share the freedom of wild animals. His increasing sense of isolation is echoed by the stormy weather and the coming of autumn.

■ Text commentary

Chapter 1

Joseph Hooper and his son, Edmund, have moved to the ugly family home – Warings – after Joseph's mother's death three months previously. Edmund is taken upstairs by his father to see his dying grandfather. Joseph Hooper is glad that the three generations are present together, but Edmund says that his grandfather looks like one of the old dead moths in his collection in the Red Room. Edmund's father, a widower after an unhappy marriage, often works away in London and there is some evidence that his son resents this. Mr Hooper announces that he is looking for a housekeeper and a friend for Edmund. Mr Hooper has unhappy childhood memories of Warings, but now that it belongs to him he hopes it will give him a sense of importance.

> The opening of the book introduces a technique which Susan Hill uses frequently: the **flashback**. This makes the start of the book a little confusing and it pays to read it several times in order to be clear. The technique is useful for giving the reader insights into the minds of the characters.

The death of Joseph Hooper's father

The book opens with events surrounding the death of Joseph Hooper's father. Edmund is taken to see the old man, who has suffered two strokes. Edmund's father thinks it will be a moving moment, with three generations together, but to the boy the old man seems dead already. A theme, introduced here, runs through the book – the connection between the old man's collection of bleached moths, the appearance of his own dying body 'bleached and grey-ish white', and the lifelessness of the living Hoopers.

Mr Hooper

Joseph Hooper is keen to find a woman to help him with his difficult relationship with his son. He tells his son that he plans to do something about getting him a friend, but Edmund feels protective about his territory and it is clear that he is likely to resent anyone who comes. He asks to see the Red Room but is refused, although he knows where the key is, and his father encourages him to go outdoors and play cricket – forgetting that he has no one to play with. Mr Hooper's marriage ended six years previously when his wife died. The marriage was not a success – he has trouble remembering what his wife looked like.

Warings

Warings was built by Mr Hooper's grandfather. It was meant to show his own rising importance, but his ambition was greater than his achievement, and over the years he had to sell much of the land he bought. Now only the house is left. Mr Hooper tries unsuccessfully to convince his son that the house is something to be proud of, but really it is a monument to unfulfilled hopes. Warings is consistently described in ways which make it clear that it has none of the usual characteristics, looks, smells or feelings of a home.

The house is ugly, tall and badly angled, like its present owners. It is built of dark-red brick, perhaps reminding us of blood. It is very isolated, surrounded by gardens filled with yew trees – traditionally found in church graveyards. Rhododendrons were planted by the first Joseph Hooper, not because he liked their flowers, but because he liked their 'substantial' look. The house is filled with massive furniture. The overall impression is of an over-large house which makes its inhabitants feel small. When he was a child Joseph Hooper hated the house, but now he is a grown man – a failure, without any strength – he has come to admire its solidity. Edmund seems to have inherited the darker side of his father's character, as reflected in his choice of a coffin-like bedroom instead of a lighter, more airy room. The housekeeper, Mrs Boland, says the house smells un-lived in, like a museum, emphasising the way the Hoopers seem like dead relics from the past.

Isolation

The Red Room

We are not told why the Red Room is so called, but the usual symbolism of red (danger, blood, fire) seems appropriate, for the room is a tomb for the moths, insects and animals within it. Even the books in the room (it was designed as a library) are like dead monuments, for they have never been opened. A great deal of importance was attached to the Red Room by Joseph Hooper's father, because it represented his fame as a collector. For Mr Hooper it represents his heritage. It comes to be important to Edmund as a means of torture for another delicate and vulnerable creature. Eventually even Mrs Kingshaw comes to admire the room, which marks the way she has virtually abandoned her ties with her son and cast her lot with Mr Hooper.

Mr Hooper

Joseph Hooper and his family

Relationships within the family have never been good, as Edmund realises when talking to his father about his relationship with Edmund's grandfather. It seems that much of Joseph Hooper's young life was spent arguing

Childhood

with his father, being forbidden to go out, having to sit and watch his father kill insects, butterflies and moths in poison-fume bottles and being lectured on how much of a failure he himself was. Joseph Hooper thinks he has failed as a father because he has never managed to ingratiate himself with Edmund. Here lies the key to their relationship – 'ingratiate' means deliberately to behave in a way which will get you into someone else's good books, so that they will think well of you. It carries undertones of insincere and shallow behaviour. Such behaviour has little to do with being a good parent.

We learn something about Edmund

Edmund steals downstairs at night – quite unafraid – to explore the Red Room he has been forbidden to enter. Unlike his father, who hates the room and the collection, he seems to feel drawn to it. The cold moonlight floods in from the window – another symbol of the colourless and chill lives the Hoopers lead – as Edmund finds the moth which excites and fascinates him the most. It seems appropriate that he feels at one with the Death's Head Hawk Moth – a symbol of hunting and death – and that it collapses into lifeless dust at his touch. He will have a similar effect on young Kingshaw.

Chapter 2

Helena and Charles Kingshaw arrive at Warings. Mr Hooper has been looking forward to their arrival, but Edmund resents the thought of someone else sharing what he sees as his house. Edmund refuses to come down from his room to meet the new arrivals and throws an unfriendly message to Charles from his window. At their first uneasy meeting alone, the two boys fight. Kingshaw is afraid and unhappy in his new surroundings. Edmund is told to show Kingshaw around and, although he begins by going out of the house, he soon returns and runs through many rooms. Kingshaw gives up trying to follow him and ends up sitting on the stairs. The boys part company in silence, and it is clear that they are not going to get on.

The Kingshaws arrive

The arrival of the 'informal housekeeper', Mrs Kingshaw, and her son is accompanied by some anxiety in Mr Hooper and his son. Edmund clearly resents the coming of another boy to 'his' house and feels that a mother – even another boy's mother – has nothing to offer him. He cannot remember his own mother.

As Edmund thinks over the implications of the Kingshaws' imminent arrival, it rains heavily, with 'great bruise-coloured' clouds hanging low. He makes a model of a barrow (an old burial mound) out of plasticine which he will later slice open. Then he will complete his map of the battle of Waterloo. These ominous references foreshadow violent events.

Hooper drops a message which says, 'I didn't want you to come here' through the window, and although Kingshaw picks it up, he does not mention it to his mother. This tells us something about his relationship with his mother, who seems preoccupied with her own appearance. We learn that Kingshaw did not want to come to the house.

The boys' first meeting

At their first meeting, Hooper taunts Kingshaw about not having a house of

Hoopcr

his own and brags about Warings and the moth collection. He tells Kingshaw that his grandfather died in the bed he will sleep in. Kingshaw feels desperate to make his mark and shows Hooper a photograph of his father who died four or five years previously. All Hooper sees is an old, 'cadaverous' man. Hooper is determined to make Kingshaw feel unwelcome. We learn that Hooper did not want to come to Warings at first, but now he is fiercely protective

of it. When Kingshaw says Hooper should shut 'his' bedroom window, Hooper attacks him and they fight.

Kingshaw's isolation

Hooper's snobbery surfaces when he makes it clear that only private schools

Kingshaw

are 'proper' schools and we learn that Kingshaw's fees are paid for him at his school. Kingshaw has come prepared to make friends and to give way on almost anything in order to do so – he feels 'too vulnerable to let himself indulge in the making of enemies'. But Hooper's behaviour puzzles him and after he leaves, Kingshaw weeps. Even though he has arrived with his mother, he feels he has nobody to talk to about his feelings, even if he could put them into words.

Hooper's isolation, and the drawing of the battle-lines

Hooper locks himself in his room, and as his father tries to get him to open

Evil

the door there are subtle suggestions of things to come: the pencil shavings which look like a moth emerging from its chrysalis, the nearly complete battle map, the childish way in which Hooper colours his drawings. These hint that battle-lines are being drawn in more ways than one and that Hooper's physical immaturity hides an unsuspected menace. Mr Hooper feels the same frustration as Kingshaw did at his failure to communicate with Edmund. He is uncertain of himself with his son and seems somehow afraid of him.

Hooper takes Kingshaw around the conservatory and loses no chance to blame him for anything that is wrong. Hooper deliberately rushes round the house, and eventually Kingshaw sits on the stairs, tired of trying to keep up. He wishes for a stream or a wood where he could be by himself. This is the first reference to the place where he eventually finds a permanent resting-place, safe from Hooper. He finds the silent menace of Hooper frightening, but is unable to take advantage of his chances to punish him.

Kingshaw

Chapter 3

A week has gone by. Kingshaw is studying a map of the countryside surrounding Warings, which he decides to explore on his own. Having walked across several fields, intending for the most part simply to get away from the house, he ends up in a cornfield close to Hang Wood. He is attacked by a huge, black crow, which follows him as he runs away. He falls over and the crow lands in the middle of his back but, after a moment or two flies off, leaving him unharmed but very shaken. As Kingshaw runs back to the house, the crow continues to follow him at a distance. On his return to the house he is confronted by Hooper, who has witnessed these events and sneers at him for being afraid of a bird. Hooper dares Kingshaw to go into the copse, or into the big wood and Kingshaw feels that he will have to do it. That night, Kingshaw awakes in his darkened bedroom and sees a thin beam of moonlight shining on something halfway down his bed. He switches on his light and sees that Hooper has left a huge stuffed crow on his bed. He turns off his light and lies in terror, afraid of wetting the bed. The next afternoon Hooper shows him the Red Room, which is full of dead animals and moths on display. Hooper sees that Kingshaw does not like the moths and locks him in the room. That night, after being let out by Mr Hooper and his mother, he remembers his school, where he feels he belongs.

Events move out of doors, now that the house and the characters who live there have set the tone of the novel. Kingshaw goes out to explore the surrounding landscape, mainly as a way of proving to himself that he can cope on his own. In contrast to the house, its inhabitants and its atmosphere, the countryside is bright with colour, bursting with life and flooded by hot sunshine.

Nature

The crow attacks Kingshaw

Into the stillness of this scene comes the great black crow which attacks

Isolation

Kingshaw, for no obvious reason. What frightens him most is the persistent way it attacks him. He feels isolated and afraid – feelings which increase as he finds it difficult to escape over the rough ground. He thinks of all the terrible stories he has read about vultures pecking out people's eyes. But the terror is all in his mind. The crow and Hooper become connected in Kingshaw's mind by the reasonless way they attack him. The crow may have been trying to drive an intruder from its territory. This is also the reason Hooper offers for his behaviour towards Kingshaw, but only at first. Soon the persecution acquires a pleasure of its own.

Hooper feels driven to persecute Kingshaw

Sensing that Kingshaw is terrified, Hooper, who has witnessed the incident,

Hooper

taunts him about being afraid. He dares Kingshaw to prove his lack of fear by going into the copse or the big wood. This is the second reference to the wood. Kingshaw has never been faced with 'such relentless persecution' and does not know how to deal with Hooper. Interestingly, Kingshaw is unaware of how frustrating Hooper finds his behaviour. One of the very few insights into Hooper's thoughts is that he finds Kingshaw's 'stone-walling' impenetrable. We wonder whether Hooper might stop if Kingshaw can only keep this up. Meanwhile, Hooper feels driven to keep trying, to 'bait and bait'.

Fear drives Kingshaw onwards

Kingshaw

Kingshaw feels driven to do things which people dare him to do. He feels driven to confront his own fear, as he did with the swimming pool ('the more afraid he had become, the more he had known he would have to jump in'). It is fear itself which drives Kingshaw on and, because his fear is always with him, he suffers permanent torment.

That night, the dead crow appears on Kingshaw's bed

Kingshaw

Hooper is clearly fascinated by this new game of tormenting someone who never fights back. Remembering Kingshaw's reaction to the crow which attacked him, he decides to get the old stuffed one from among the dusty relics in the attic. Kingshaw is expecting Hooper to torment him somehow. When he finds the stuffed crow on his bed, he knows at once who has put it there. As with his fear inside, his knowledge about the crow – that it is not alive – only seems to make it worse. He feels powerless to touch the crow. Because it is a psychological war, neither boy speaks of the incident the following morning. Kingshaw knows that he must never let Hooper know what he is thinking. Their behaviour is misunderstood by Mr Hooper and Mrs Kingshaw, who are convinced the two boys are getting along famously.

Kingshaw is locked in the Red Room

Kingshaw

Hooper shows Kingshaw the Red Room. The 'dead' smell frightens him and he becomes terrified when he realises that the display cases contain dead moths. Kingshaw has been afraid of moths since childhood. Again his fear is rooted in what they *might* do to him and although he knows the moths are dead, his own imagination terrorises him. Hooper senses this and locks him in the room alone. As rain pours down, Kingshaw realises that darkness is falling and panic overtakes him. The shadows of the trees in the garden remind him of men, watching him, lying in wait. When he is finally released, instead of blaming Hooper he says nothing. He feels so isolated that he bears the truth alone, goes upstairs and is violently sick. One of the tragedies of Kingshaw's life is the number of occasions on which he could have stopped everything simply by telling his mother what was happening. How much notice she would have taken is open to question.

Love

Kingshaw yearns to be back at school

Later that night, Kingshaw hopes that they will not stay at Warings. He

Kingshaw

comforts himself with the thought that it will soon be time to go back to school and he will be away from Hooper. By the end of the next term they may be living somewhere else, as has happened frequently before. Kingshaw is happy at school, where he has been for nearly four years and where he feels safe. He feels that he does not need to keep beginning again at school because 'he had become the person they had all decided that he would be'. School represents his only stability. It is the nearest thing he has had to a proper home for a long time.

Chapter 4

A week has passed. Kingshaw finds a room at the top of the house which seems to be unused. A postcard comes from Devereux, one of Kingshaw's school friends. Hooper is determined to find Kingshaw's secret room. Mr Hooper finds some boardgames and the boys play together, but without friendship. Hooper finds Kingshaw's hideaway and realises that Kingshaw is planning to run away because he is afraid of him. The relationship between Mr Hooper and Mrs Kingshaw develops, and they think that the two boys are also getting along.

Kingshaw finds the empty room

After almost three weeks in the house, Kingshaw finds an empty room in a

Kingshaw

remote part of the top corridor. The room appeals to him because it seems to have 'no character of its own' and he feels he 'might be able to take it over'. He enjoys being alone there, and feels safe. He finds other people unpredictable, although he regrets that he was not permitted to go on holiday with his school friends. It is clear that his mother's real reason for refusing him permission was that she wished to have him with her. He discovers that he

actually hates Hooper now and is frightened of his own feelings.

Hooper is determined to find the room

Evil

Mr Hooper finds his son impossible to understand. He can remember when he was Edmund's age, hating his own father, and this thought makes him uncomfortable. Meanwhile, Hooper plots a search of every room in the house to find Kingshaw's hideaway. We might wonder whether the spirit of evil which Susan Hill has said inhabits Hooper may not have more in common with the gruesome

creature described in his horror comic: 'formed at the dawn of history...'

Kingshaw plans to run away

Meanwhile, Kingshaw plans his escape. He thinks that even if the attempt

Kingshaw

Mrs Kingshaw

fails, the others will understand why he did it. This shows that Kingshaw's plan to run away is as much a desperate attempt to communicate as it is an impulse to escape from Hooper. Whatever its cause, he feels he has no choice: 'it was necessary, that was all.' As before, once Kingshaw accepts his own fear, he has to go through with whatever it is that causes the fear: though frightened of running away, he will not now change his mind.

Kingshaw does not like the way his mother has changed and become 'eager' around Mr Hooper. For her part, she desperately does not want him to do anything which might spoil what she sees as her 'chance' in life.

The adults assume that because the two boys play draughts and bagatelle together, they are firm friends. This shows the gulf separating the adults' world from the boys.

In fact, the boys' game is a fierce battle and parallels their other, more dangerous, contest of wills. Ominously, their struggle takes place against a darkening sky and heavy rain.

Hooper will go with Kingshaw

When Hooper discovers Kingshaw's secret room, he quickly realises

Evil

Kingshaw's intention to run away. He is, however, momentarily outmanoeuvred when Kingshaw challenges him to tell the adults, because he has no proof of anything. Hooper contents himself with taunting Kingshaw that nothing in the house belongs to him and that he has therefore stolen the things he has collected. Finally, he announces that he will accompany Kingshaw when he runs away. We might have thought that Hooper would be satisfied to have driven Kingshaw away, but Hooper's real purpose is clearly to be Kingshaw's relentless torturer. Kingshaw realises there is no possibility of a truce, but he also knows he cannot stay: the changes in his mother upset him, and he hates the house – everything inside it seems dead.

A twist in the tale

Mr Hooper

Ironically, just as Kingshaw is planning to leave, Mr Hooper is planning to mark the changes he sees in his own life. He plans to redecorate Warings, clear out the attics, throw parties for friends and make contact with the locals. The adults are so overjoyed at the changes in their own lives that they are blind to the events taking place between their children.

Chapter 5

Kingshaw's mother announces that she is going to London with Mr Hooper for a day. Kingshaw realises that this is a chance to run away, because they will leave early in the morning and return late. He decides to go across country, to avoid being seen. At about five o'clock the following morning he leaves the house with a rucksack of provisions, makes his way through the cornfield where he met the huge crow, and skirts round the edge of Hang Wood, looking for a way in across the ditch and through the fence. Noticing a wart on the back of his middle finger, he remembers the tales told by his school friends about people who got rid of warts by wishing them onto somebody they do not like. Eventually he finds a gap at the far end of the wood, and goes in.

Kingshaw runs away

Mrs Kingshaw is going to London to buy things for the cocktail party Mr

Mrs Kingshaw

Hooper has decided to give. They seem uneasy with each other, like children: she is over-enthusiastic and he gives a 'shy smile'. She is also shy, and blushes when Mr Hooper invites her into the sitting-room. The comment about the boys enjoying 'a bit of an adventure' in the absence of the adults is ironic: we later learn that Kingshaw regards it as anything but an adventure.

Although Mrs Kingshaw 'worried a good deal about her capacity for motherhood', motherhood for her seems to entail saying the right things and looking at ease, rather than showing love and understanding.

Isolation

Notice the subtle touches which show the isolation experienced by each of the characters. Mrs Kingshaw is going to travel with Mr Hooper, but for the rest of the day he will be at work; Kingshaw has plenty of money because he is always given it for Christmas and birthdays. Nobody takes enough interest in Kingshaw to find out what presents he might like, and he gets more money 'because he hadn't got a father'.

Kingshaw's preparations for running away show his resourcefulness. He realises there is not much point in struggling to take water when it is likely that there will be streams. Compare Kingshaw's preparations with Hooper's.

Kingshaw

When Kingshaw wakes up he wonders about his mother and whether he 'ought to care' about her. He reminds himself that she doesn't care about him – she seems convinced he is 'settling down so happily'. Notice that Kingshaw is unsurprised by his mother's lack of understanding. Kingshaw continually reminds himself that everything he does will fail. This can seem confusing, because he is determined to try almost anything to make friends or, eventually, to escape. The key to this is that Kingshaw is driven by fear of what might happen to him. He is permanently anxious about threats, especially imagined ones, the 'terrible possibilities'. In the face of physical danger, he often shows courage.

Men on the moon

As Kingshaw leaves the house behind, it vanishes into the mist like a bad

Nature

dream. Surrounded by the silence of nature, he presses on until the tractor 'looms' suddenly out of the mist, like something in a lunar landscape. This is a reminder that Susan Hill wrote the book during 1969, when the first moon landing took place. The tractor looks out of place in the landscape, like the machines and rubbish left by the first

35

lunar landing. The world of nature has little in common with the world of man. Notice how Kingshaw's fears are what *might* happen. He is afraid of the tractor and of beasts which *might* have eaten half-moon shapes out of the corn at the edge of the wood. In fact, it was probably deer, too shy to enter the field, which ate the corn.

Kingshaw feels proud of himself

Kingshaw is pleased with what he has done, as though he is unused to showing initiative. But anxiety mars this small moment of triumph when he notices the wart on his hand. Kingshaw naturally assumes that he has the wart because someone does not like him. Closing his eyes, he steps into Hang Wood.

Uncover the plot

Delete two of the three alternatives given, to find the correct plot. Beware possible misconceptions and muddles.

Edmund Hooper and his father move to Moorings/Warings/Farings three/four/five months after the death of the boy's uncle/grandmother/grandfather. The house is very ugly (made of brick/granite/concrete outside and mainly of elm/oak/beech inside), and is surrounded by elm/oak/yew trees. Edmund is fascinated by the Red/Green/Black Room, where the collection of butterflies/moths/stuffed animals is kept. Charles Kingshaw arrives with his mother, who is to act as housekeeper/cook/maid, and Edmund immediately makes his life a misery. During his first/second/third venture outside, Hooper/Kingshaw/Fielding is attacked by a raven/eagle/crow; his tormentor, observing this, places a stuffed model of the bird on his bed/desk/pillow that night. The following day, Hooper locks Kingshaw in the Red Room, where he is very uncomfortable/excited/frightened. Kingshaw adopts the conservatory/playroom/kitchen as his own and makes his model of a battlefield/barrow/galleon there, planning to run away. Hooper threatens to tell the adults/destroy his model/to follow him. The adults go to London/Manchester/Birmingham for the day and Kingshaw leaves the house at 5am; it is cold/warm/hot and clear/rainy/misty. After walking for about an hour, he crosses a ditch/stream/fence and enters Hang Wood.

Who? What? Why? When? Where? How?

1 Who cooks and cleans for Mr Hooper?
2 Who sends a postcard to Kingshaw and from where?
3 What is the name given to Edmund's grandfather's collection?
4 What five things does Kingshaw take into Hang Wood, apart from food?
5 Why is Kingshaw frightened of his bedroom?
6 Why does the Death's Head Hawk Moth disintegrate?
7 Where does Kingshaw keep his money hidden?
8 Where is the key to the Red Room kept?
9 How old are Edmund and Charles?
10 How long is Kingshaw at the house before he begins to explore the surrounding countryside?

Who is this?

1 Who 'was a freak, he was so bad at everything'?
2 Who 'thought about school.... It was safe'?
3 Who was 'very tall and thin and dark, like a crow'?

Familiar themes

The theme of death is important in this novel; both boys have a dead parent; Kingshaw thinks that Hooper is dead twice; by the end, he himself is dead. The discussion that the two boys have in Hang Wood (Ch 7) is centrally important, and revealing of both characters.

1 Which two deaths are referred to on the first page of the novel?
2 What is Edmund's reaction to the collection of moths? What was his father's? What is Kingshaw's?
3 Apart from the moths, what other dead animals are to be found in the Red Room? What other stuffed animal is important in the plot?
4 What dead things and natural violence do the boys come across in the wood?
5 Which images of death are associated with the farm and what is Fielding's attitude to them?

Prove it!

Find a quote from the text that could be used to back up each of the following statements. (The numbers in brackets refer to the chapter you might like to look up in the commentary for help.)

1 Hooper is pale and does not like going outdoors (4)
2 Kingshaw would rather be outside than indoors (2)
3 Mrs Kingshaw worries a lot (2 or 5)
4 Mr Hooper is often nervous or alarmed (1 or 2)
5 Neither of the boys feels close to his sole remaining parent (1 and 5)

Self-test (Answers) Chapters 1–5

Uncover the plot

Edmund Hooper and his father move to Warings three months after the death of the boy's grandmother. The house is very ugly (made of brick outside and mainly of oak inside), and is surrounded by yew trees. Edmund is fascinated by the Red Room, where the collection of moths is kept. Charles Kingshaw arrives with his mother, who is to act as housekeeper, and Edmund immediately makes his life a misery. During his first venture outside, Kingshaw is attacked by a crow: his tormentor, observing this, places a stuffed model of the bird on his bed that night. The following day, Hooper locks Kingshaw in the Red Room, where he is very frightened. Kingshaw adopts the playroom as his own and makes his model of a galleon there, planning to run away. Hooper threatens to follow him. The adults go to London for the day and Kingshaw leaves the house at 5am; it is cold and misty. After walking for about an hour, he crosses a ditch and enters Hang Wood.

Who? What? Why? When? Where? How?

1 Mrs Boland (1)
2 Devereux (a friend from school; from Norfolk (4)
3 Lepidoptery (1)
4 A torch, a penknife, some sticking plaster, a pair of socks and a ball of string (5)
5 Because Hooper tells him that his grandfather died there (2)
6 Because Hooper touches it (1)
7 In a navy-blue cotton bag inside a Lego box (5)
8 In the left-hand drawer of Mr Hooper's desk (1)
9 Both are nearly eleven (2)
10 Over a week (3)

Who is this?

1 Leek (5)
2 Kingshaw (3)
3 Mr Hooper (5)

Familiar themes

1 The deaths of Edmund's grandmother and grandfather
2 Edmund is 'fascinated by them, excited', while his father hated the collection, but dared not say so and rebel. Kingshaw is frightened of live moths, and equally, if irrationally frightened of the dead ones (note the frighteningly named Death's Head Hawk Moth).

3 In Chapter 1, a stuffed stag, a grey fish, a weasel, a stoat and a fox are mentioned. Hooper places a stuffed crow on Kingshaw's bed
4 a The dead rabbit. Kingshaw likes the feel of it until he notices the maggoty wound in its ear. Later, Kingshaw catches a rabbit, but cannot bring himself to kill it.
   b Kingshaw catches a fish but again cannot bring himself to kill it; he leaves it to die
   c Hooper watches a thrush 'banging a snail down on to a flat stone to smash the shell'.
   d At night: 'An owl came, with an ominous, swift whirring of its wings... Earlier, they had watched a sparrow hawk overtake a small bird, in mid-air, reaching out and pulling it back with its claws, and then gripping it to death as it flew on.'
5 The calf that Fielding and Kingshaw watch being born is to be killed for veal; Fielding describes how he catches the turkeys' decapitated heads in a dustbin at Christmas. His attitude is straightforward, practical and unimaginative, unlike that of the sensitive Kingshaw

Prove it!

1 'Joseph Hooper had rarely gone out, and never been allowed to strip off his shirt, and so had been very pale. Now, his own son was pale' (4)
2 'I would like to get right away from Hooper, I would like to find a stream or a wood by myself' (2)
3 'Mrs Helena Kingshaw wore a jade green suit and worried about it, lest it should be thought too smart' (2); or 'she worried a good deal about her capacity for motherhood, about whether she said the right things and looked sufficiently at ease...' (5)
4 ' "You must not be afraid", [Edmund's] father said, nervously ...'; or 'Joseph Hooper... was suddenly alarmed at the arrival of this woman, alarmed by what he had done' (2)
5 '[Mr Hooper] said, "I shall be away in London a good deal. I cannot live here the whole time, even in your holidays." "That won't be anything new, will it?" (1); and ' "Charles is settling down so happily", (his mother) had said, and Kingshaw had been appalled, hearing it, though not really surprised. She had never known anything about him, he had never wanted it' (5)

Chapter 6

Kingshaw discovers that he likes the sounds and sights of the wood. Hearing a sound, he hides behind a holly bush and sees Hooper through the trees. Hooper has followed him, as he said he would. Kingshaw's feelings of happiness at being in the wood are completely spoiled. In a small clearing, the boys discover a deer and follow it. After a while, Kingshaw realises they are lost.

Inside Hang Wood

Kingshaw likes the wood because he feels hidden in its innocence. The rabbit

Nature

he sees thrills him because, unlike the ones at school which have 'vacant eyes', it 'quivered and twitched with life'. The school rabbit is like the dead one Kingshaw finds in the next chapter, its eyes 'glazed, blank and distant'. Kingshaw's desire for freedom is echoed by the freedom of woodland animals. The wood is in many ways a frightening place, but for Kingshaw it represents escape from his own fear, from Hooper, from his mother, from the house and from everything else which hems him in. Even the approach of some unknown thing through the bushes does not frighten him.

Why has Hooper followed Kingshaw?

Kingshaw feels frustrated when Hooper appears. He cannot understand why

Hooper

Hooper should want to follow him: 'you don't like me'. Hooper gives no reason, he just smiles. He torments Kingshaw simply because of the pleasure it gives him. This realisation produces a 'churning and boiling' inside Kingshaw's head.

Kingshaw has come to see Hooper as something almost inhuman. He is therefore surprised when they stop – because they hear animal sounds – and he sees Hooper's sweat. Not for the first time he asks himself what Hooper can actually do to hurt him. But physical threat is not the issue, because in spite of his memories of terrible animals, Kingshaw is the one who moves forward to investigate the noise.

The boys follow the stag and become lost

Significantly, it is Hooper who takes over the role of hunter when they

Isolation

discover that the mysterious noise is a stag. He says that he knows all about how to stalk things and is an expert at 'what hunters do'. Hooper criticises Kingshaw at every opportunity. Interestingly, in view of his criticism of Kingshaw as being stupid for not bringing something to drink, Hooper declares that there are always streams in woods. In fact, it is Kingshaw who has the practical mind.

He notes anxiously the passing of time and realises that they have become lost. Kingshaw's reaction is to stop and think what to do, whereas Hooper 'crumples'.

Chapter 7

A thunderstorm is coming. Hooper becomes afraid and says storms make him sick. Kingshaw makes a shelter out of his anorak as Hooper is transfixed by terror. After the storm, the boys find a stream. Kingshaw finds a dead rabbit, and the boys talk about what happens when animals and people die. They follow the stream until it emerges at a pool in a clearing. The boys undress and swim in the pool until the sun goes in. They become cold and decide to light a fire. It becomes clear that they are not in Hang Wood as Kingshaw thought, but in the much larger Barnard's Forest. Hooper becomes hysterical at the thought that no one will find them. Kingshaw goes to see if they are near the edge of the forest whilst Hooper is to catch a fish. As he explores, Kingshaw catches a rabbit, but cannot kill it. He considers not going back for Hooper, but eventually returns to find him face-down in the water, having slipped and banged his head. Kingshaw rescues him and lights a fire as Hooper revives. Kingshaw takes care of Hooper as night begins to fall.

Hooper is terrified of the storm

Hooper

Kingshaw is unable to take advantage of Hooper's terror. This is a notable difference between the two boys. Hooper's reaction to the storm is not rational – he suggests that they could 'run for it' even though they have been in the wood for hours. It is clear that Hooper is a coward.

Kingshaw feels sympathy for Hooper

Kingshaw does not feel frightened by the wood, but freed by it. He thinks

Love

it has brought him to the edge of 'discovering some secret'. He gets busy constructing a shelter from his anorak as Hooper watches, trembling with fear. Kingshaw knows what it is to be afraid, to want 'to tear his way out of himself', and so he is sympathetic to Hooper. Hooper never feels sympathy for Kingshaw, however much he torments him. This emphasises his inhuman nature, his evil. After the storm, Hooper behaves as though nothing has happened.

The dead rabbit

The difference between the two boys is underlined when Kingshaw discovers and nurses the dead rabbit. Hooper has no time for dead animals or dead people, they 'are finished' and 'don't matter'. He seems genuinely

Nature

astonished that anyone might think differently. Hooper mockingly asks Kingshaw if he believes 'all that guff about souls and ghosts and everything' and Kingshaw replies: 'not ghosts'. Unlike Kingshaw, Hooper does not believe that people have souls. Hooper cannot imagine what having a soul means because there he has no goodness, kindness, sympathy or pity.

They find the stream

After Hooper's comments, Kingshaw throws the maggoty rabbit away. It has become revolting to him. They immediately discover the gloomy, weed-clogged gully in which runs the stream. The woods, initially a source of mystery and beauty are (now that Hooper has arrived) an airless, dirty jungle, smelling 'sweetish and rotten' with decay. Nothing lives in the dark, damp gully. Even Hooper finds it 'funny' and 'creepy'. But Kingshaw presses on, because he likes 'to get to the end of things'. Again, we see that his way of coping with fear is to push deeper into it.

They find the pool

They find a pool and the sun comes out, so the two boys swim. Kingshaw

Kingshaw

feels relaxed and free in the pool. When it turns cold they leave the water, and Kingshaw is the practical, organised one. He has brought plasters, says they should make a fire and have something hot to eat. Hooper seems helpless and becomes threatening when Kingshaw, in getting him organised, pushes his luck too far. Again, Kingshaw realises that Hooper's fear is of outside things, like the thunderstorm, whereas Kingshaw's fear is within.

Hooper becomes hysterical and Kingshaw looks for a way out

Hooper becomes hysterical at the thought that they will never be found.

Hooper

Kingshaw is forced to slap his face hard, after which Hooper cries for a long time and then is sick. He is further terrified when Kingshaw suggests tying the string to a tree and walking off to see if they are near the edge of the wood. Hooper is obviously frightened of being left, but Kingshaw goes exploring anyway and manages to catch a rabbit. When he sees the terror in its eyes he knows he cannot kill it, and sets it free. What do you imagine Hooper would have done?

Kingshaw finds himself unable to desert Hooper

Kingshaw realises that if he walks on and leaves Hooper he will be free, like the rabbit. But he feels somehow responsible for Hooper and returns to find Hooper face-down in the stream. He has hit his forehead on a rock in the

Kingshaw

stream and is unconscious. This incident strengthens Kingshaw's feeling that he would have been somehow guilty of killing Hooper if he had not come back. Kingshaw lights a fire and takes care of Hooper, who threatens to kill him if he 'finds the way out' by himself. This is nonsense on one level, because if Kingshaw escapes Hooper will not have the opportunity to kill him. But, in another way, Hooper does eventually 'kill' him, as the only 'escape' Kingshaw finally finds is suicide.

Chapter 8

It grows dark. Kingshaw catches a fish but is unable to kill it and so leaves it on the ground to die. He tries to cook the fish but the inside is raw and they can eat only a little. Hooper torments Kingshaw with the idea that his mother came to Warings with the intention of marrying Mr Hooper. Because Kingshaw partly agrees with this it makes him angry. Darkness falls and Hooper sleeps, watched over by Kingshaw, who eventually falls asleep but is awakened by Hooper screaming for his mother in a nightmare. Kingshaw slaps Hooper to waken him, then gets him some water. Hooper says that when they are found he will put the blame on Kingshaw. Hooper becomes feverish and Kingshaw gives him his jumper to add to the anorak he has already given him. Hooper makes Kingshaw promise not to leave him, although Kingshaw is maddened by Hooper's weakness and complaints.

Darkness falls

As darkness falls, Hooper brags about the expensive watch his father will buy him for Christmas. As with almost everything else Hooper says, this is intended to hurt Kingshaw. Kingshaw caught a fish and tried unsuccessfully to cook it. This becomes something else Hooper attacks him about. Notice how Kingshaw is unable to kill the fish but leaves it to die, and how he cannot bring himself to cut the insides out to cook it properly.

Kingshaw's feelings about his mother

Hooper taunts Kingshaw about the way his mother always comes to kiss him

Mrs Kingshaw

good night, but becomes afraid when it looks as though Kingshaw might hit him. He gloats over Kingshaw again by asking if his mother has 'gone after' many other men. What hurts Kingshaw most is that he knows there is some truth in what Hooper is saying and he is stung by his own memories of how his mother looked at speech days and how embarrassed he was of her. Hooper is matter-of-fact about Mrs Kingshaw's behaviour – he feels that it's what people do if they need money and a house. This passage neatly illustrates Kingshaw's sense of frustration at his mother's behaviour and Hooper's callous behaviour.

Hooper has a nightmare

Kingshaw lies awake in the darkness, frightened by the noises of the wood.

Isolation

He feels that he would be safe if only he could cover himself with a blanket. He feels alone – that no one will want to come and get them. He falls asleep but is woken by Hooper, screaming about how something is unfair, begging someone to stop, crying that he has got the blazer. Although Hooper's cries are difficult to interpret, they may well be about him being bullied at school. He also cries out for his mother. Perhaps, long ago, Hooper was once an ordinary little boy, someone who like Kingshaw was afraid of being bullied and who needed his mother. Kingshaw frequently calls him a baby, and he sleeps with his thumb in his mouth. Again, Kingshaw is forced to hit Hooper.

Kingshaw will be blamed for everything

Evil

Hooper makes it plain that when they are found he intends to blame Kingshaw for them being in the woods and for getting lost. In spite of this, Kingshaw promises not to leave Hooper alone. He even feels he has to reassure Hooper that he wouldn't really hurt him – again, he gives away the advantage he has over Hooper. Hooper frustrates Kingshaw and makes him afraid of his own emotions, particularly of the way he wants to hurt Hooper.

Chapter 9

The boys awaken early. Hooper feels better but has a bruise on his forehead, where he fell. Kingshaw goes for a swim in the stream whilst Hooper watches a thrush breaking a snail's shell open. They hear shouting and dogs barking as a search party approaches.

Nature

The wood is a timeless, peaceful place

Kingshaw feels that they have been in the wood for years. Everything outside the wood seems far away. This feeling of escape and release draws Kingshaw back to the wood, later in the novel.

Hooper

The thrush and the snail

Kingshaw goes for a swim, while Hooper watches a thrush banging a snail on a flat stone. Just like the snail, Kingshaw retreats into his shell of silence to avoid Hooper's persecution. But, like the thrush, Hooper knows that perseverance will destroy Kingshaw's defences. Perhaps this is why Hooper watches the thrush so intently. The sight of the thrush destroying the snail fascinates Hooper in the same way as his own persecution of Kingshaw.

Has the wood really changed anything?

Kingshaw

Kingshaw does not want to be found and his peace spoilt. He feels happy, because not even Hooper can torment him in the wood. For Kingshaw the wood has made everything different, and he hopes that everything will be all right from now on.

Chapter 10

Hooper tells his father and Mrs Kingshaw that Kingshaw pushed him into the water and kept hitting him. Kingshaw is angered by these lies and by the way the adults seem to believe them. He is frustrated by the way Hooper seems to have gained advantage from the incidents in the wood. As Kingshaw is sent from the room in disgrace, Hooper kicks him. Later, when Kingshaw is in bed, his mother talks to him about the events in the wood. It seems clear that she completely fails to understand the situation between the two boys. She thinks it important that her son get on well with everyone in the house and appears to be on the brink of telling Kingshaw something, but stops short. After she leaves, Kingshaw realises that his mother and Mr Hooper are going to marry, and that Hooper will become his brother.

Kingshaw is blamed for everything

Isolation

Evil

Back home, Hooper fulfils his promise and blames Kingshaw for everything, who is furious to discover that the adults seem happy to believe every word. Again, all the attention seems to go to Hooper. No one bothers to ask Kingshaw why he ran away, which is ironic as one of his reasons for doing it was to try to communicate with the adults. Even this has failed. Kingshaw feels that he could kill Hooper. He cannot understand why the adults believe such obvious lies. He realises that it is because they know nothing about him. He feels betrayed by his mother. Kingshaw feels lonelier in the house than he did in the forest and he realises that Hooper is completely evil.

Mrs Kingshaw seems to have no time for her son

Mrs Kingshaw is full of sympathy for Edmund and almost ignores her own

Mrs Kingshaw

son, whom she seems to blame for everything. She makes no attempt to comfort him but fusses over Edmund and supports Mr Hooper in sending her own son to his room in disgrace. Kingshaw feels that he would like to spit in Mr Hooper's face. He sees Mr Hooper as some kind of 'terrible bird' persecuting him.

Kingshaw is depressed by his conversation with his mother

Kingshaw feels trapped and the events in the wood seem distant now – 'the

Isolation

house was taking over again'. He tried to escape, but Hooper has dragged him back again. He feels that his mother is becoming like Mr Hooper, siding against him. They even have the same expression in their eyes now when they look at him. When she comes upstairs to talk to him he realises that, although she does not say it in so many words, she is going to marry Mr Hooper. He also realises that she understands nothing about the real relationship between him and Hooper. Again, the chance is lost for Charles to tell his mother what is happening and how he feels.

Chapter 11

At breakfast, Mr Hooper announces that after the holiday Kingshaw is to attend Drummonds, Hooper's school. Kingshaw hides inside a dark shed in the allotment but Hooper follows him and locks him in. He becomes frightened inside the shed, is sick but eventually sleeps, only to be awakened from a nightmare about a Punch and Judy show by the sound of his name being called. Hooper has come to torment him, and threatens to leave Kingshaw locked in the shed. He says that when Kingshaw comes to his school he will make his life miserable because he has lots of friends. He frightens Kingshaw with ideas about the kinds of insects and animals that might be in the shed. Later, Hooper returns and unlocks the shed to tell him that it is lunch time and that they are all going somewhere with his father.

Evil

Kingshaw is to go to Edmund's school

The news that Kingshaw is to attend Drummonds is so dreadful to him that he feels he must find somewhere out of Hooper's reach. He runs into the garden and hides in a shed at the bottom of the allotment. Hooper found his secret room but now he has another place where he can be by himself. But Hooper follows him and locks him in.

Kingshaw is trapped like a wild animal

Kingshaw becomes frightened at all the awful things which might happen to

Kingshaw

him. He wonders if it was not Hooper who locked him in after all, but someone else. He remembers the terrifying stories in the horror-comics he read at school, where 'your eyes went on and on' until you had nightmares. After beating uselessly on the sides of the shed in panic he tries to spread sacks on the floor, but something terrifies him as it runs across his hands. Screaming, he beats his hands against his trousers until he is sure it has gone. His hands are now slimy. He is sick, them sleeps on some straw.

Kingshaw's ordeal inside the shed

Kingshaw dreams a nightmare about a Punch and Judy show on a moon-like

Childhood

beach of dusty sand, full of schoolboys. Punch's skull breaks open; Judy's body heaves up and down; the shrieking noise becomes that of a crow and the puppets turn into crows which circle above. The nightmare is a jumble of recent events in Kingshaw's life. Kingshaw awakens to hear Hooper's voice taunting him from outside. Hooper is indifferent to Kingshaw's screams and in reply to Kingshaw's questions says he might have locked him in because he felt

like it, or perhaps because he wants to make him 'go away'. This is a telling comment, because if Hooper had really wanted Kingshaw to go away he

Evil

would have let him, rather than have followed him into the wood. He tells Kingshaw no one will find him. He will tell everyone that Kingshaw has gone back into the wood. Anyway, he says, Kingshaw's life is going to be miserable at school because Hooper will make all the other boys be horrible to him, although – typically – Hooper's threats are vague because he knows that this will frighten Kingshaw more. For the same reason he tells Kingshaw that there

might be rats, moths or bats inside the shed. Kingshaw despairs and screams that he will kill Hooper, but when there is no reply, he weeps. After a long time he hears the sudden approach of footsteps, and Hooper lets him out and

Hooper

runs off. Hooper seems determined to imprison Kingshaw whenever he can – either within the house or in the shed, but always within his own fear. Psychologically, Hooper will never let him go: he seems well-named in that respect.

In the house, Hooper tells the adults they have been playing at bandits. Kingshaw walks slowly back to the house and the weather seems to echo his mood, as the sky weeps large spots of rain, like sweat.

■ Self-test (Questions) Chapters 6–11

Uncover the plot

Delete two of the three alternatives given, to find the correct plot. Beware possible misconceptions and muddles.

Kingshaw/Hooper/Fielding likes the wood; he sees a wild rabbit, which runs/bumps/flashes away. Hearing a noise, he hides behind a yew/oak/holly tree, but Hooper discovers him and follows. A deer/goose/wolf barks/honks/howls at them and they follow it, becoming lost. Hooper is terrified by the prospect of being lost for ever/starving/a thunderstorm; the boys find a river/pool/stream and talk about death/life/memories. Kingshaw manages to catch a fish/rabbit/vole but lets it go; while Hooper is trying to catch a fish/rabbit/vole, he falls and hurts his arm/leg/head and Kingshaw rescues him. Hooper has a nightmare and becomes feverish/chilled/sick, but the boys are rescued.

Back at home, the adults blame Hooper/Kingshaw/themselves. Kingshaw's memory of how things were in the wood fades/becomes clearer/vanishes. He is horrified when his mother/Hooper/Mr Hooper announces that he is to attend St Vincent's/Warings/Drummond's school with Hooper. He hides in the attic/the shed/the conservatory but Hooper locks him in and he has a terrible nightmare about a Punch and Judy show/a fair/a circus.

Who? What? Why? When? Where? How?

1 Who lent out bloodbath books at 2d for four days at Kingshaw's school?
2 To whom does Hooper cry out in his nightmare?
3 What does Hooper feed to the thrush?
4 With what does Kingshaw make a shelter from the storm?
5 Why do the adults blame Kingshaw for the episode in the wood?
6 Why, according to Hooper, did Kingshaw's mother come to the Warings?
7 When is Kingshaw let out of the shed, and by whom?
8 Where is the dead rabbit's 'great mealy wound'?
9 How does Kingshaw's nightmare in the shed end?
10 How much, according to Hooper, is his new watch going to cost?

Who is this?

1 Who 'pulled his knees tight up to his belly'?

2 Who 'went right back into the farthest corner, where it was dark, and curled up tightly, his hands held up towards his face'?
3 Who 'felt that he was on the brink of discovering some secret, of whose existence, even, that other world did not know'?

Who says?

1 Who says: 'There are things I see that you don't'?
2 Who says: 'I didn't get a fish, I almost did... you needn't think I didn't try, only I couldn't keep it, it slipped, I couldn't...'?

Parallel lines

Compare the following events in the novel, which echo and contrast with each other.

1 Hooper and Kingshaw's first encounter, and Kingshaw's first encounter with Fielding
2 The two incidents in which Kingshaw saves Hooper and tries to save him
3 The two incidents in which Hooper locks Kingshaw in
4 In Chapter 1, Hooper declares 'I am never afraid'. In Chapter 10, Kingshaw tells his mother 'I'm not frightened of anything now'. In Chapter 16, Fielding says 'I'm not frightened of much.' Whom do you believe?
5 Kingshaw's two visits to the stream in the wood

Stormy weather

The central characters are often frightened, anxious, nervous or unsure of themselves. This atmosphere of dread is mirrored in the hot and thundery weather and in the dark, claustrophobic interior of the Warings. Find quotes to prove the following statements.

1 Before the thunderstorm in Hang Wood, Kingshaw feels a great tension in the natural surroundings (7)
2 Mrs Boland's efforts to let light and air into Warings are not successful (1)
3 It is even airless in Hang Wood, following the stream (7)
4 – and at Leydell Castle (12)
5 Rain fails to lighten the atmosphere – e.g. when Kingshaw is released from the shed (11)

■ Self-test (Answers) Chapters 6–11

Uncover the plot

Kingshaw likes the wood; he sees a wild rabbit, which bumps away. Hearing a noise, he hides behind a holly tree, but Hooper discovers him and follows. A deer honks at them and they follow it, becoming lost. Hooper is terrified by a thunderstorm; the boys find a stream and talk about death. Kingshaw manages to catch a rabbit but lets it go; while Hooper is trying to catch a fish, he falls and hurts his head and Kingshaw rescues him. Hooper has a nightmare and becomes feverish, but the boys are rescued. Back at home, the adults blame Kingshaw. Kingshaw's memory of how things were in the wood fades. He is horrified when Mr Hooper announces that he is to attend Drummond's school with Hooper. He hides in the shed but Hooper locks him in and he has a terrible nightmare about a Punch and Judy show.

Who? What? Why? When? Where? How?

1 Ickden (1)
2 His dead mother. (8)
3 Crumbs of biscuit (9)
4 His anorak (7)
5 They feel Kingshaw instigated the project and Hooper only followed (10)
6 To ensnare Mr Hooper as her husband (8)
7 At lunchtime, by Hooper (11)
8 In its ear (7)
9 All the puppets turn into crows, which take off and circle overhead (11)
10 Over £50 (8)

Who is this?

1 Kingshaw (11)
2 Hooper (7)
3 Kingshaw (7)

Who says?

1 Hooper (8)
2 Hooper (7)

Parallel lines

1 Both these first encounters demonstrate jostling for position and recognition. Both Hooper and Fielding begin abruptly and Kingshaw is put on the defensive, but comes back fighting his corner. At a certain point, Hooper becomes menacing and concedes nothing, while Fielding shows Kingshaw how to knot plantains and shoot the heads off. From that, a shared game begins and the friendship flourishes, while Hooper rejects the possibility of shared fellow-feeling.

2 In the first incident, Kingshaw pulls Hooper bodily out of the stream, giving Hooper his own sweater and anorak to keep warm. His only thought is to save Hooper and he blames himself for leaving him. When Hooper is unable to move up the wall of Leydell Castle, he tries immediately to help him and suddenly realises his own power, but does not yield to the temptation. When he reaches a hand to help Hooper, the other boy thinks it is to push him.

3 Hooper locks Kingshaw in the Red Room and in the shed. On both occasions, Kingshaw is terrified and afraid of the dark and claustrophobia. In neither instance does he give Hooper the satisfaction of hearing him beg or cry out

4 Fielding is instantly believable and his claim is very matter-of-fact. Unlikely as Hooper's claim is, with its absolute 'never', Susan Hill tells us it is true. Kingshaw's claim is obviously untrue but is perhaps his way of denying the fear he feels and holding on to his pride.

5 On both occasions, he is intensely happy. Previously, he has been scared of swimming, but here he feels in control, natural and he enjoys the feeling of the water. At the end of the novel, he revisits the place where he felt so much himself and again takes off his clothes to feel the silky smoothness of the water. There is no distress in the description of his suicide.

Stormy weather

1 'There was a feeling of tension inside the wood, as the sky darkened.... Kingshaw was hot. He wanted the storm to break, he wanted rain and coldness.... he felt everything around him to be holding back some kind of violence' (7)

2 'Mrs Boland... had gone about trying to let in light and fresh air, where she could. But Derne was low-lying, and the air that summer was close and still' (1)

3 'It smelled steamy and damp, like a jungle, and there was another smell, too, sweetish and rotten. There was no air....' (7)

4 'But even up here, it was warm and airless' (12)

5 'Outside, great, flat spots of rain began to fall heavily, one by one, like sweat from the sky...' (11)

Chapter 12

They all visit the ruins of Leydell Castle. Kingshaw decides to climb and dares Hooper to follow him. Having got as high as he can, Kingshaw turns round to see Hooper, who has climbed onto a ledge some way below him. He reaches Hooper, who cannot move because he is afraid. As Kingshaw reaches out his hand to help, Hooper flinches and falls to the ground.

A trip to Leydell Castle

Childhood

Kingshaw's forced enthusiasm for the trip is noticeable, as she is 'ready to be full of interest and admiration'. At first Kingshaw does not like the place because it reminds him of his dream, but he feels happier once he starts to climb the walls. Typically, Hooper is content to amuse himself destructively, by digging his initials into the stone with a pen-knife.

"I'm The King of The Castle"

Kingshaw feels elated as he climbs higher, in spite of the increased danger,

Kingshaw

because he is safe from the others. He feels free, as though he 'might touch the sky', and feels he is the 'King of the Castle' (King-shaw?). This echoes the old rhyme, 'I'm the King of the Castle, and you're a dirty rascal', but we know that Hooper is much more than a childish rascal. Kingshaw has a good head for heights and taunts Hooper. Climbing was something he was distinguished in at school, being the only person ever to reach the crow's nest at the top of the elm tree above South Gate. He shouts obscenities at his mother and Mr Hooper – saying what he really feels, thinking only Hooper can hear him. He dares Hooper to follow him.

Why does Hooper climb after Kingshaw?

It seems that Hooper is driven to pursue Kingshaw and we might wonder

Hooper

what purpose he hopes to achieve by trying to follow Kingshaw up the castle walls. He might want to belittle Kingshaw by showing him that he cannot achieve anything for himself. Try to decide what you think Hooper's reasons are, as you did about Hooper's reasons for following Kingshaw into the wood. In both cases Hooper is afraid of what he does, so his reasons must be strong. Each time, Kingshaw asks him outright why he has come, but Hooper cannot explain.

Hooper falls from the castle walls

Typically, Hooper blames Kingshaw for his difficulties, and is clearly terrified: he wets his pants and will not open his eyes. Even though Kingshaw is in a position to destroy his enemy, as usual he feels unable to take advantage of it. In reaching out to help Hooper, he frightens him and Hooper falls.

Chapter 13

Kingshaw is driven back to Warings by his mother. During the journey he remembers a school prefect, Lesage, who used to send Kingshaw on pointless errands, feed him chocolate and make him lie on the floor. During one assembly, Lesage read out a passage about the soul flying from the body. Kingshaw wonders whether Hooper's soul has flown from his body: he is convinced that the fall has killed Hooper. Mrs Kingshaw returns to the hospital, leaving her son with the housekeeper at Warings. That night Kingshaw wakes from terrible nightmares and runs downstairs looking for his mother. He finds Mr Hooper and his mother, who explain that Hooper is not dead. Mr Hooper carries him back up to bed.

Kingshaw sees Hooper fall in what seems like slow-motion. In the moment

Isolation

of silence after Hooper hits the ground, Kingshaw feels like a bird or a god, above everyone. He is appalled at his own calmness as everyone else rushes around. From behind the hills the thunder rumbles, a reminder of the previous storm in the woods. Like the wart which appeared on his hand, Kingshaw feels sure that Hooper has been killed because he, Kingshaw, wished it to happen. He assumes that everyone else will think this too.

Kingshaw remembers Lesage

Kingshaw remembers an assembly at school where Lesage, who was Deputy

Childhood

Senior Prefect, read out a passage about the soul flying from the body. Remember that when the boys talked in the woods, Kingshaw said he believed that people have souls (though Hooper dismissed the idea as 'guff'). Lesage used to send Kingshaw on long, pointless errands at school and once made him lie down on the floor with his eyes closed whilst he stood over him. He remembers being disturbed by this incident and being unable to make any sense of it.

This bizarre scene may be another example of how Kingshaw is psychologically dominated by others.

Mrs Kingshaw

Mrs Kingshaw is concerned

Kingshaw tries without success to explain to his mother, as she drives him home, that he did not push Hooper. She seems lost in her own thoughts, as though more concerned about the possibility that the accident could damage her relationship with Mr Hooper. Kingshaw tells her that it is being afraid which makes you fall. This is an insight into his own character: Kingshaw knows all about the power of fear. But he gives up when it becomes clear that, as usual, she is not listening to him.

We get a rare glimpse of Mrs Kingshaw's feelings towards her son when she asks him to promise never to do anything like this again. She seems genuinely worried that it might have been him and says she worries about him all the time. Kingshaw is alarmed, sensing her panic. Her concerns are very 'proper' and her behaviour is very 'correct', but Kingshaw is aware that there is no love or warmth in her for him.

Love

Kingshaw thinks about life without Hooper

Kingshaw is left with the housekeeper, Mrs Boland, who is watching

television. At first he is fascinated by the dancing girls on the screen, but then a film begins which frightens him because of its threatening images and music. He goes to the kitchen to escape. When he gets to his room he thinks of the future. If Hooper is dead then he, Kingshaw, will be 'King of the Castle' at Warings, and might not have to go to Hooper's school. He longs for his own school as he falls to sleep and the nightmare begins.

Kingshaw

Kingshaw's nightmare

Kingshaw dreams of clawing hands dragging him back down a tunnel

through which he is escaping to the light. He is surrounded by great beating wings, crows, puppets with bleeding heads and ambulance men. Escape seems near, and he knows he will be safe when he reaches the end of the tunnel. As he reaches the daylight he runs across a field, then falls from a cliff into the sea. The nightmare is a mixture of terrifying experiences from his past and contains a premonition of his future death by drowning.

Isolation

Hooper is not dead

As Kingshaw runs downstairs looking for his mother, he remembers Hooper

crying out in terror for his own mother in the wood. It is Mr Hooper who eventually answers Kingshaw's noisy crying, and who takes him downstairs for a hot drink. There, his mother and Mr Hooper comfort him but it takes an effort even then to get them to understand why he is upset. He learns that Hooper is not dead after all. Mr Hooper carries him back to bed and, although Kingshaw's descriptions of him so far have been filled with images of

Love

paleness and predatory birds (especially crows), he is comforted by being carried and wants it never to end. He feels overcome by shame, gratitude and relief. Later, he feels ashamed at behaving in this way with Mr Hooper, and cannot sleep, now that he knows Hooper is not dead after all.

Chapter 14

Mrs Kingshaw goes to visit Hooper in hospital. Kingshaw tells his mother that he wishes Hooper had been killed. He remembers how one boy, Fenwick, behaved when he had a bad fall at school. During Hooper's absence Kingshaw makes a model of a helter-skelter. Mrs Kingshaw and Mr Hooper tell each other that children often say things they do not mean and that they are sure the boys will get on perfectly all right. Kingshaw explores the surrounding countryside and wanders into the church, where he meets Fielding, a local boy. They play together and Fielding invites Kingshaw to look around the farm where Fielding lives. Kingshaw watches a calf being born, sees some turkeys and is allowed to hold Fielding's pet hamster. Kingshaw is invited to stay for dinner and Fielding offers to lend him his bike so he can go and ask if he can stay. When Kingshaw gets to Warings his mother tells him that Hooper will be home the following day. Later, Kingshaw tells Fielding some of his problems. Fielding thinks Kingshaw allows everyone to boss him about too much. Kingshaw later learns that Hooper will not be home the following day, after all.

Mrs Kingshaw goes to visit Hooper in hospital

Kingshaw is doing one of Hooper's jigsaws as his mother prepares to visit

Childhood

Hooper in hospital. She insists that he send Hooper a message and seems determined to believe that the two boys are friends. Kingshaw is still ashamed at the way he cried for her and thinks of what Fenwick, a boy at school, would have said. Fenwick had a bad fall, but was determined to be brave and show little pain. Kingshaw wishes he could be more like that. As his mother pesters him to send Hooper a present, Kingshaw tells her that he wishes he had been killed, after which she goes away. He feels happy on his own and warms himself in the sunshine, remembering how he had made a model helter-skelter the previous week.

Mrs Kingshaw

Mrs Kingshaw convinces herself that there is nothing to worry about and puts her son's comments down to 'a little bit of shock and hysteria after the accident'. She is comforted by Mr Hooper, who thinks that 'children will always get along'. Hooper feels pleased that Mrs Kingshaw comes to see him because, even though he does not like her, he thinks it means she would rather be with him than with her own son.

Kingshaw meets Fielding

Kingshaw goes out in the sunshine to explore. In the church, he remembers

Fielding

the way he wished bad things would happen to Hooper and worries about how 'bad thoughts always came back on you'. He remembers the wart still on his left hand. He kneels down suddenly and prays to God, saying he is trying to be sorry, but is interrupted by a local boy, who tells him he shouldn't be there. As he leaves the church two magpies fly off, startled, and the boy follows him. They begin to chat and the boy invites Kingshaw to his home to see their new turkeys. He seems to know a lot about Kingshaw and is surprised when Kingshaw asks him his name. He introduces himself as Fielding. This is another example of a character having an appropriate name: Fielding is the son of a local farmer.

Nature

When they arrive at Fielding's farm, Kingshaw is invited to watch a cow calving. He does not feel that this is given to him as a test, or that Fielding will laugh at him – for Fielding is very different to Hooper – but he is anxious. It is the potential danger which worries him. Afterwards he finds himself overwhelmed by the experience. He is envious of Fielding's relaxed manner and the way he is at 'ease, in the face of the physical'. He becomes upset

when Fielding tells him about how young turkeys are killed. Fielding is used

Love

to the everyday violence of farming, whereas Kingshaw is bewildered by so many 'terrible truths'.

Fielding's mother is welcoming and natural and Kingshaw wishes his own mother was the same. He feels as though he has found a place where he can be himself. Fielding lends him his bike to go and ask permission to stay for tea, but when he reaches Warings his mother tells him that Hooper is due home from hospital the next day.

Fielding tries to help Kingshaw

Kingshaw tells Fielding about his problems with Hooper, who seems to

Fielding

understand them, but not why Kingshaw cannot solve them. He tells Kingshaw that he shouldn't let other people boss him about so much. Kingshaw envies Fielding's self-confidence. He feels proud and happy when he finds Fielding's tortoise and is delighted next day when he learns that Hooper cannot come home from hospital yet. Perhaps Fielding was right, and Hooper will not be able to return to school straightaway.

Chapter 15

Hooper returns and accuses Kingshaw of using his things in his absence. The old hostility between them returns. Kingshaw remembers being beaten up at school by a bully, Crawford, and he is afraid that this may happen when he goes to Hooper's school. To get away from Hooper, Kingshaw goes to the shop for an ice-cream. On the way back he meets Fielding, who is going with his father to market. They are taking the calf which Kingshaw saw being born – it is to be sold for veal. Later, Hooper tells him he knows about Kingshaw's friendship with Fielding. Mr Hooper takes Kingshaw to London to buy the uniform for his new school. When they return to Warings, Hooper is playing with the model fort which Kingshaw made. When Kingshaw complains about this, Mr Hooper strikes him across his face. Kingshaw goes to Hooper's bedroom and demands his model back. Hooper throws it across the room and breaks it. Kingshaw's mother appears in the doorway and tells her son that he should be ashamed of himself.

Hooper comes back from hospital

Evil

As soon as Hooper gets back, the old animosity starts up again. Hooper seems to know that Kingshaw has borrowed his jigsaw puzzle and he accuses him of being a thief. Kingshaw is weary of this constant battle, with everything he does being criticised. Even his mother seems determined to torment him. Hooper taunts him about all the visits Mrs Kingshaw made to see him and the presents she gave him. Kingshaw is surprised at how much he minds this. He realises that what happened in the past was only a beginning and that things with Hooper will now be worse.

Kingshaw remembers being bullied at school

Childhood

Mrs Kingshaw

Hooper tells Kingshaw that something will happen to him and Kingshaw thinks this is probably true – he expects to be punished for all his bad thoughts about Hooper. Kingshaw now dreads the start of every day. He remembers a school bully called Crawford, who had hurt him. To Kingshaw, Hooper's threats are more frightening because they are unspecific. On his way out to see Fielding, his mother calls him back. He makes an excuse that he is going to get an ice-cream, and notices that his mother speaks to him differently now; she seems sharper and more impatient. He feels that she is doing it to please Mr Hooper. Because of his age, Kingshaw does not understand why Mr Hooper is being so generous to them, like paying for him to go to a new school. In the past his mother told him that other people do not understand how hard it is for them, but Mr Hooper seems different.

Hooper knows about Fielding

In the village Kingshaw meets Fielding, going to market with his father to sell

Fielding

calves for veal, including the one Kingshaw saw being born. Although he is invited to go with them to market, he is afraid of the 'new terrors' he will find there, like seeing the calves led away for slaughter. But if he goes he could be with Fielding and away from Warings. He feels frustrated because he both wants and doesn't want to go. Back at the house, Hooper tells him he knows all about Fielding, and that Mrs Kingshaw tells him lots of things about her son.

Kingshaw goes for his new school uniform

Mr Hooper takes Kingshaw to London for his school uniform. On the train,

Mr Hooper

Kingshaw wonders why everything always has to change and why, as usual, the changes seem to have nothing to do with what he wants. Mr Hooper finds it easier to deal with Kingshaw than with his own son, because there is 'nothing strange about him', and he feels a new confidence. Ironically, he thinks he understands boys very well now and that they 'are very simple animals'. Looking back, Mr Hooper convinces himself that his painful childhood memories are

exaggerated and that he had been happy really. Contrast this with his thoughts at the start of the book.

It has 'all begun'

Isolation

Mr Hooper recites the names of streets and places in London. He forgets, in spite of Kingshaw's reminder, that the boy used to live in London and therefore knows it well. Kingshaw considers running away, but he finds the city more frightening than Hang Wood. He looks in a mirror and sees himself in the uniform of Hooper's school. He realises that it has 'all begun'.

Hooper breaks Kingshaw's model fort

Evil

Back at Warings, Kingshaw is furious to discover that his mother has given Hooper the model fort which he built. Kingshaw feels that the two adults do not want him to have anything of his own. He feels that there is no place for him. When he complains, Mr Hooper strikes him across the face. Although she is shocked, his mother also looks relieved.

Chapter 16

Helena Kingshaw receives a telephone call from an old girl friend. During the call she says she has not quite made up her mind about the future. Mr Hooper and Kingshaw overhear this part of the conversation. Later, Kingshaw wonders whether they are going to stay at Warings. He remembers a hotel where they once stayed, the worst place they have been. He particularly disliked one guest, Mrs Mellitt. Recalling the telephone conversation, Mr Hooper wonders whether he has been decisive enough in his relationship with Mrs Kingshaw. Kingshaw realises Hooper is unhappy about the likelihood of Mr Hooper marrying Mrs Kingshaw. The following day they all go out in Mr Hooper's car for a surprise. Kingshaw becomes afraid when they arrive at a circus, because the thought of it has always made him feel ill. On the way out, he is violently sick. Later, Mrs Kingshaw tells her son that she has invited Fielding to tea. When Fielding comes to Warings, Hooper shows him the Red Room. Kingshaw is resentful of this, and refuses Fielding's invitation back to his farm. Whilst Hooper is visiting Fielding, Kingshaw destroys Hooper's battle maps.

A telephone call

Mrs Kingshaw receives a telephone call from her old friend Enid Tyson and,

Mrs Kingshaw

knowing that Mr Hooper can hear what she says, tells Enid that she has not quite decided what to do about her future. She says this in the hope that it will push Mr Hooper into a decision about asking her to marry him. With unintentional irony, she tells Enid that her son Charles is a changed boy. She describes Charles' relationship with Edmund as having a few 'little upsets and frustrations', but that they are both very happy. Kingshaw is also listening, but he mistrusts her words because he detects a slight overemphasis in what she says. However, his hopes rise a little. Perhaps they will not always be at Warings after all.

Kingshaw remembers Miss Mellitt

Kingshaw

Kingshaw remembers some of the other terrible places they have stayed, especially one hotel where he met Miss Mellitt. Miss Mellitt did nothing threatening, but because she seemed mysterious to Kingshaw, he found her frightening. He felt uncomfortable looking at her bits of bald scalp and pink skin and remembers that it was her smell which bothered him most.

Mr Hooper decides he has waited long enough

Mr Hooper

Mr Hooper is also turning over Mrs Kingshaw's words in his mind. Her ploy seems to have worked, because he concludes that he has been indecisive. He seems to see Mrs Kingshaw in terms of his own sexual needs, and feels disturbed at seeing her every day. His previous wife permitted him limited sexual freedom. Since her death, his only sexual outlet has been erotic imaginings about girls on the Underground there, or provocative pictures outside erotic cinemas. He thinks he recognises similar sexual desires in Mrs Kingshaw and that she will willingly fulfil his sexual fantasies.

Hooper is angry about his father's coming marriage to Mrs Kingshaw

Hooper tells Kingshaw that he knows that his father is going to be Kingshaw's

Isolation

step-father. Although Hooper brags about this, Kingshaw realises that Hooper is angry about the coming marriage. But instead of feeling glad that Hooper minds, Kingshaw feels nothing but isolation. Later that night, he realises he will never be able to escape Hooper. He cries when he thinks of staying forever in that terrible house with its dead moths and old furniture, and with Mr Hooper in his mother's room.

The circus

Mr Hooper arranges a surprise trip to the circus. Hooper gloats in triumph

Isolation

as he realises that Kingshaw hates being there. Mrs Kingshaw is preoccupied with looking after Edmund and virtually ignores her own son, even though she knows that circuses frighten him. Mr Hooper buys expensive seats close to the ring, but Kingshaw is terrified of the noises and smells. He feels pity for the animals and almost weeps at the docile expressions in the eyes of the gentle elephants. He feels that, like him, they are trapped, humiliated and helpless.

Mr Hooper is bored – he has only come for the sake of the boys – until the female trapeze artists appear. Then he becomes aroused, and feels for Mrs Kingshaw's knee. The circus and the night's events make Kingshaw violently sick, but his mother only scolds him.

Kingshaw goes to the clearing

Mrs Kingshaw tells Charles that she has been to see Mrs Fielding. Kingshaw

Nature

is angry because if Fielding comes to Warings he will meet Hooper and will no longer be his exclusive friend. He goes alone to a place he knows and likes, where the squirrels play and leap freely about in the trees. But this time, there are no squirrels. Kingshaw knows that Fielding will not be afraid of Hooper, but he feels sure that he will lose Fielding's friendship. For Kingshaw, 'that was the last thing'.

Fielding visits Warings

When Fielding comes to Warings, it is as Kingshaw had feared. Fielding is alarmed by the animosity between the two boys, especially by Kingshaw's

Fielding

behaviour. Kingshaw thinks it is unfair that Hooper knows he cannot make Fielding afraid, but always knew he could make Kingshaw afraid. Kingshaw tries to think of an explanation for this, but does not realise that evil people such as Hooper will persecute anyone they can. When faced with strength, Hooper will always back down. Fielding touches the dead animals in the Red Room and looks at the dead moths. He is unafraid and clearly finds the room uninteresting. Kingshaw recalls that even his mother is now in favour of keeping the terrifying things in the room. She seems to have changed and he wonders whether things were not better before they came to Warings. But then he remembers how she used to cling to him, and how he could not bear 'the weight of meaning' in her words.

Fielding and Hooper go to the farm

Fielding

Hooper suggests they go to the attics, and Kingshaw realises that Hooper wants to find the stuffed crow. Kingshaw's temper flares when Hooper taunts Kingshaw, saying he daren't go. To defuse the tension, Fielding suggests that they all go back to his farm to see the new tractor. In spite of repeated invitations, Kingshaw stays at the house, even though he wants to go more than anything else. Fielding is concerned that his friend is upset, but Hooper dismisses Kingshaw's behaviour, saying he is always like that.

Kingshaw destroys Hooper's maps

Kingshaw goes to Hooper's bedroom, collects his maps, takes them outside and destroys them. Realising what he has done, Kingshaw knows that the remaining five days before the wedding and before the boys go to school, do not bear thinking about.

Chapter 17

The house is full of suitcases as preparations are made for leaving. That night, a note appears under Kingshaw's bedroom door, telling him that something will happen to him. When he awakens early the following morning, Kingshaw leaves the house and goes to the pool in the wood. He undresses and lies in the water, puts his head under the surface and takes 'a long, careful breath'. His body is found by Hooper, who feels triumphant that Kingshaw has drowned himself because of him.

Time to go

Suitcases are packed as preparations are made for the wedding and for the boys to go to school. Mr Hooper twitches with desire at the thought of the honeymoon in Torquay. Kingshaw is anxious because Hooper has done nothing since he destroyed the battle maps. In the psychological battle between the boys, Hooper knows that not retaliating makes Kingshaw more afraid.

'Something will happen to you, Kingshaw'

Isolation

Kingshaw looks round his bedroom that night. It is bare, just as it was when he first arrived. His mother spends a long time with him, because she knows he will be leaving her the next day. Later that night, Kingshaw is woken by a sound and finds the message under his door: 'Something will happen to you, Kingshaw'. He knows it is from Hooper, and when he sleeps his dreams are full of nightmares again.

Kingshaw leaves Warings for ever

Kingshaw

Kingshaw wakes at dawn and realises what he must do. It reminds him of the last time he ran away. He walks through the fields full of stubble after the harvest, and the first shades of autumn tinge the trees at the edge of the wood. The summer is over. Kingshaw feels excited at being in the one place he feels he belongs, and where he is safe.

Plenty of time for everything

Mrs Kingshaw

Back at Warings, Hooper lies in untroubled sleep, whilst his father has excited dreams. When Mrs Kingshaw wakes she feels her troubles are over. Her words echo those Kingshaw used to describe his terror at starting at Hooper's school: 'everything is about to begin'. They are true in a way she does not understand. She thinks there is plenty of time for everything now, not realising that for her son there is almost no time left. As Kingshaw realised, he has never understood anything.

Kingshaw reaches the pool

Kingshaw

Kingshaw undresses by the pool. He hesitates only a moment, thinking about all the things which Hooper has done in the past and may do in future. He thinks about the new school and his mother's wedding and realises that there is nothing left for him now. He has no choice. He lies face down in the water and drowns.

Hooper is triumphant

Evil

Hooper finds Kingshaw's body because he instinctively knows where it will be. He feels triumphant. Mrs Kingshaw tells him not to look, in case he is upset. She has no real understanding of what has happened to her son, nor of Hooper's nature; she is determined that 'everything is all right'.

Afterword

Susan Hill explains how she came to write the book in 1969 and how far the events of the time might have influenced her work. She describes her feelings about the characters, considers whether she might have written it differently, and talks about why she does not fully understand it herself.

Where was the book written?

Susan Hill wrote the book in a beautiful corner of Dorset, in the year that men first landed on the moon (1969). Although the beauty of her surroundings inspired the setting for the story, the plot itself came later.

Childhood

One day she watched two boys playing together. The boys were grandchildren of the local farmer and struck her as two typically English prep-school boys. This is echoed in both the material of the story – the details about the schools of Kingshaw and Hooper, the slangy way the boys often speak – and in other touches, like the way the boys are often referred to by their surnames. This also makes them seem more 'distant' as characters. But the two boys Susan Hill saw were happy friends.

Where did the story come from?

Susan Hill is unsure where the dark side of the boys in her book came from,

Evil

especially Hooper, whom she thinks evil. Susan Hill knows that other authors have written about the cruelty of children towards each other, but suspects that Kingshaw and Hooper come from her own character and past – an area which, as a writer, she leaves unexplored for fear that her inspiration will vanish if she over-analyses it.

Although the book is about children, Susan Hill wrote it for adults. But young people understand it better than adults. Young people appreciate that Kingshaw's suicide is not as far-fetched as some adults would like to believe. The book's realism helps to make events more believable – such as the boys' use of swear words.

Why did she write the book?

Susan Hill says of the three characters alive at the end of the book: 'But God

Love

help the trio of survivors'. They are isolated from reality and from each other, although the adults have convinced themselves otherwise. Susan Hill says she does not altogether understand the book herself, and accepts that many people dislike it, but says that her purpose is that of any writer – to make people feel they are not alone. For some people, the events in the book are all too real.

■ Self-test (Questions) Chapters 12–17

Uncover the plot

Delete two of the three alternatives given, to find the correct plot. Beware possible misconceptions and muddles.

They visit a circus/a zoo/a castle and Kingshaw climbs the wall; at school, he was the only person to reach the crow's/eagle's/thrushes' nest at the top of the yew/elm/oak tree. Hooper, following him, falls, and Kingshaw watches it happen as if in slow motion/in a film/in a dream. He is happy/sad/terrified, thinking that Hooper is dead. After his nightmare, he is comforted by Mr Hooper/Mrs Boland/his mother but later feels shame/guilt/fear for this. He thinks of Lesage's/Fenwick's/Leek's bravery at school and is anxious/desperate/curious to know how Hooper felt; left to himself, he is happy/lonely/fearful. He meets Fielding in a church/barn/field and they watch the birth of a hamster/dog/calf. When he asks his mother if he can stay to lunch/tea/dinner, he learns that Hooper is to come home the next day/that week/in a week. All the old friendship/competitiveness/hostility returns and Hooper breaks Kingshaw's model of a barrow/fort/galleon. Hooper/Kingshaw/Mrs Boland is particularly upset by the marriage plans of the adults. A surprise visit to a zoo/circus/castle makes Kingshaw faint/cry/sick and he loses Fielding as a friend all to himself. The morning before he is to go to school, Kingshaw goes to the pool/river/stream and drowns himself. Hooper feels triumphant/guilty/full of remorse at what he has caused to happen.

Who? What? Why? When? Where? How?

1 To whom does Kingshaw call out in his nightmare?
2 Who was Deputy Senior Prefect at Kingshaw's school?
3 What causes Hooper to fall from the castle wall?
4 What does Kingshaw find that belongs to Fielding?
5 Why does Mr Hooper take Kingshaw to London?
6 Why do you think Kingshaw is so frightened of the circus?
7 When does Hooper urinate in fear in this section of the novel?
8 Where does Kingshaw vomit in fear in this section of the novel?
9 How does Kingshaw kill himself?
10 How does Kingshaw pass the time while his mother is visiting Hooper in hospital?

Who is this?

1 Who 'smiled at him, and then looked away again, peeling potatoes'?
2 Who 'had smelled oddly musty, like clothes left for years in a chest of drawers'?
3 Whose 'face was very small, and brown as a nut'?

Who thinks?

1 Who thinks: 'I'm the King of the Castle, now. I can do *anything*'?
2 Who thinks: '...it was because of me, I did that, *it was because of me*'?

Echoes

The last chapter provides echoes of earlier incidents, adding to the feeling of inevitability – but there is a new sense of relief and escape. Where in the novel are the following echoed?

1 Hooper's note to Kingshaw (2)
2 Hooper's triumph at Kingshaw's suicide (4)
3 Mrs Kingshaw's obsession with clothes (2)
4 'The nightmares began' (2)
5 The last sentence: 'Then, there was the sound of men, splashing through the water' (9)

Prove it!

Both adults in the novel fail to provide the love and understanding that the children need so desperately and they share in the blame for Kingshaw's suicide. Susan Hill, however, gives insights into their lack of confidence and confusion. Find a quotation from the text that could be used to back up each of the following statements.

1 Mr Hooper lacks confidence in his parenting ability (1)
2 Mrs Kingshaw lacks confidence in her parenting ability (5)
3 Mr Hooper is inconsistent in his attitude to children. Find two conflicting thoughts he has on the subject (4 and 15)
4 Kingshaw and Hooper both reject overtures of love or interest from their parents (2 and 10)

Self-test (Answers) Chapters 12–17

Uncover the plot

They visit a castle and Kingshaw climbs the wall; at school, he was the only person to reach the crow's nest at the top of the elm tree. Hooper, following him, falls, and Kingshaw watches it happen as if in slow motion. Hooper is terrified, thinking that Hooper is dead. After his nightmare, he is comforted by Mr Hooper but later feels shame for this. He thinks of Fenwick's bravery at school and is curious to know how Hooper felt; left to himself, he is happy. He meets Fielding in a church and they watch the birth of a calf. When he asks his mother if he can stay to dinner, he learns that Hooper is to come home the next day. All the old hostility returns and Hooper breaks Kingshaw's model of a fort. Hooper is particularly upset by the marriage plans of the adults. A surprise visit to a circus makes Kingshaw sick and he loses Fielding as a friend all to himself. The morning before he is to go to school, Kingshaw goes to the stream and drowns himself. Hooper feels triumphant at what he has caused to happen.

Who? What? Why? When? Where? How?

1 His mother (13)
2 Lesage (13)
3 Kingshaw stretches out his hand to help him and, thinking he means to push him, Hooper flinches in terror and falls (12)
4 Archie, his tortoise (14)
5 To buy his new school uniform (13)
6 Partly he feels claustrophobic in the tent; partly the noise and the forced merriment overpower him. Mainly it is pity for the animals (16)
7 Climbing the wall at Leydell Castle (12)
8 At the circus (16)
9 He drowns himself by deliberately breathing in water (17)
10 He does a jigsaw (14)

Who is this?

1 Fielding's mother (14)
2 Miss Mellitt (16)
3 Fielding (14)

Who thinks?

1 Kingshaw (12)
2 Hooper (17)

Echoes

1 The note in Chapter 17 reads: 'Something will happen to you, Kingshaw'. In Chapter 2, Hooper drops a note to Kingshaw before he even meets him: 'I didn't want you to come here'
2 Hooper's final feeling of triumph is pre-echoed when he realises Kingshaw is planning to run away, 'I know why you're doing it as well. It's because of me. You're scared of me...' (4)
3 There are many examples of this. In Chapter 2, she worries in case her jade-green suit is thought too smart
4 The nightmares Kingshaw experiences in the final chapter echo those Hooper causes him by telling him that his grandfather died in his bedroom. There are many nightmares in the novel
5 This sentence is similar in feeling to that at the end of Chapter 9: 'When he opened his eyes again, his view of the tree-tops and the sunlight was blocked, by a man's head'

Prove it!

1 '...he knew that he had failed, from the very beginning, to ingratiate himself with Edmund' (1)
2 '...she worried a great deal about her own capacity for motherhood, about whether she had got the right things and looked sufficiently at ease, in his presence' (5)
3 'We cannot fathom the minds of young children' (4)
4 '"I'm quite all right. There isn't anything wrong at all." "For he hated his father to talk to him in that way, wanted to stop his ears to keep him out" (2) 'She was sitting right up to him on the bed. He could feel her weight, the shape of her thighs, if he stretched his foot out. He moved away a little' (10)

■ Writing an examination essay

Take the following to heart

- *Carefully study each of the questions set on a particular text* Make sure you understand what they are asking for so that you select the one you know most about.
- *Answer the question* Obvious, isn't it? But bitter experience shows that many students fail because they do not actually answer the question that has been set.
- *Answer all the question* Again, obvious, but so many students spend all their time answering just part of a question and ignoring the rest. This prevents you gaining marks for the parts left out.

The question

1 Read and understand every word of it. If it asks you to compare (the similarities) and/or contrast (the differences) between characters or events, then that is what you must do.
2 Underline all the key words and phrases that mention characters, events and themes, and all instructions as to what to do, e.g. compare, contrast, outline, comment, give an account, write about, show how/what/where.
3 Now write a short list of the things you have to do, one item under the other. A typical question will only have between two and five items at most for you to cope with.

Planning your answer

1 Look at each of the points you have identified from the question. Think about what you are going to say about each. Much of it will be pretty obvious, but if you think of any good ideas, jot them down before you forget them.
2 Decide in what order you are going to deal with the question's major points. Number them in sequence.
3 So far you have done some concentrated, thoughtful reading and written down maybe fifteen to twenty words. You know roughly what you are going to say in response to the question and in what order – if you do not, you have time to give serious thought to trying one of the other questions.

Putting pen to paper

The first sentences are important. Try to summarise your response to the question so the examiner has some idea of how you are going to approach it. Do not say 'I am going to write about the character of Macbeth and show how evil he was' but instead write 'Macbeth was a weak-willed, vicious traitor. Totally dominated by his "fiend-like queen" he deserved the epitaph "this dead butcher" – or did he?' Jump straight into the essay, do not nibble at its extremities for a page and a half. High marks will be gained by the candidate who can show he or she has a mind engaged with the text. Your personal response is rewarded – provided you are answering the question!

As you write your essay *constantly refer back to your list of points* and make sure you are actually responding to them.

How long should it be?

There is no 'correct' length. What you must do is answer the question set, fully and sensitively in the time allowed. Allocate time to each question according to the percentage of marks awarded of it.

How much quotation or paraphrase?

Use only that which is relevant and contributes to the quality and clarity of your answer. Padding is a waste of your time and gains not a single mark.